Survi

GLOBAL POLITICS AND

Volume 65 Number 1 | February–Marˌ

'Russian territory has served as a sanctuary for Moscow in the Ukraine war. Chinese territory would probably not be a sanctuary in a war with the United States. Short of an outright and foolish Taiwanese declaration of independence, Beijing should be deterred from attacking Taiwan by the prospect of conventional war with the United States and Japan.'

Hans Binnendijk and David C. Gompert, Towards Nuclear Stewardship with China, pp. 18–19.

'The fierce desire for rapid change seems to be taking priority over the integrity of the forms and institutions of democracy, with an increasing tolerance for authoritarian practices to address hardships and willingness to accept trade-offs between political rights and socio-economic benefits.'

Irene Mia, Can the New Left Deliver Change in Latin America?, p. 50.

'Order is fragile because it is subject to unilateralism and hegemony by dominant powers and vulnerable to disruption by the less powerful. A system is fragile because it is at odds with unrestrained sovereignty and nationalism.'

Cesare Merlini, Kissinger and Monnet: Realpolitik and Interdependence in World Affairs, p. 133.

Survival

GLOBAL POLITICS AND STRATEGY

Volume 65 Number 1 | February–March 2023

Contents

On the cover
Luiz Inácio Lula da Silva speaks at a rally in São Paulo, Brazil, on 30 October 2022 after being elected for a third term as the country's president.

On the web
Visit www.iiss.org/ publications/survival for brief notices on new books on Russia and Eurasia, Africa and Asia-Pacific.

***Survival* editors' blog**
For ideas and commentary from *Survival* editors and contributors, visit www.iiss.org/blogs/ survival-blog.

Survival
GLOBAL POLITICS AND STRATEGY

The International Institute for Strategic Studies

2121 K Street, NW | Suite 600 | Washington DC 20037 | USA
Tel +1 202 659 1490   Fax +1 202 659 1499   E-mail survival@iiss.org   Web www.iiss.org

Arundel House | 6 Temple Place | London | WC2R 2PG | UK
Tel +44 (0)20 7379 7676   Fax +44 (0)20 7836 3108   E-mail iiss@iiss.org

14th Floor, GBCorp Tower | Bahrain Financial Harbour | Manama | Kingdom of Bahrain
Tel +973 1718 1155   Fax +973 1710 0155   E-mail iiss-middleeast@iiss.org

9 Raffles Place | #49-01 Republic Plaza | Singapore 048619
Tel +65 6499 0055   Fax +65 6499 0059   E-mail iiss-asia@iiss.org

Pariser Platz 6A | 10117 Berlin | Germany
Tel +49 30 311 99 300   E-mail iiss-europe@iiss.org

Survival Online www.tandfonline.com/survival and www.iiss.org/publications/survival

Aims and Scope *Survival* is one of the world's leading forums for analysis and debate of international and strategic affairs. Shaped by its editors to be both timely and forward thinking, the journal encourages writers to challenge conventional wisdom and bring fresh, often controversial, perspectives to bear on the strategic issues of the moment. With a diverse range of authors, *Survival* aims to be scholarly in depth while vivid, well written and policy-relevant in approach. Through commentary, analytical articles, case studies, forums, review essays, reviews and letters to the editor, the journal promotes lively, critical debate on issues of international politics and strategy.

Editor **Dana Allin**
Managing Editor **Jonathan Stevenson**
Associate Editor **Carolyn West**
Editorial Assistant **Charlie Zawadzki**
Production and Cartography **Alessandra Beluffi, Ravi Gopar, Jade Panganiban, James Parker, Kelly Verity**

Contributing Editors

William Alberque	Chester A. Crocker	Melissa K. Griffith	Irene Mia	Karen Smith
Målfrid Braut-Hegghammer	Bill Emmott	Emile Hokayem	Meia Nouwens	Angela Stent
	Franz-Stefan Gady	Nigel Inkster	Benjamin Rhode	Robert Ward
Aaron Connelly	Bastian Giegerich	Jeffrey Mazo	Ben Schreer	Marcus Willett
James Crabtree	Nigel Gould-Davies	Fenella McGerty	Maria Shagina	Lanxin Xiang

Published for the IISS by
Routledge Journals, an imprint of Taylor & Francis, an Informa business.

About the IISS The IISS, a registered charity with offices in Washington, London, Manama, Singapore and Berlin, is the world's leading authority on political–military conflict. It is the primary independent source of accurate, objective information on international strategic issues. Publications include *The Military Balance*, an annual reference work on each nation's defence capabilities; *Survival*, a bimonthly journal on international affairs; *Strategic Comments*, an online analysis of topical issues in international affairs; and the *Adelphi* series of books on issues of international security.

SUBMISSIONS

To submit an article, authors are advised to follow these guidelines:

- *Survival* articles are around 4,000–10,000 words long including endnotes. A word count should be included with a draft.
- All text, including endnotes, should be double-spaced with wide margins.
- Any tables or artwork should be supplied in separate files, ideally not embedded in the document or linked to text around it.
- All *Survival* articles are expected to include endnote references. These should be complete and include first and last names of authors, titles of articles (even from newspapers), place of publication, publisher, exact publication dates, volume and issue number (if from a journal) and page numbers. Web sources should include complete URLs and DOIs if available.
- A summary of up to 150 words should be included with the article. The summary should state the main argument clearly and concisely, not simply say what the article is about.

- A short author's biography of one or two lines should also be included. This information will appear at the foot of the first page of the article.

Please note that *Survival* has a strict policy of listing multiple authors in alphabetical order.

Submissions should be made by email, in Microsoft Word format, to survival@iiss.org. Alternatively, hard copies may be sent to *Survival*, IISS–US, 2121 K Street NW, Suite 801, Washington, DC 20037, USA.

The editorial review process can take up to three months. *Survival*'s acceptance rate for unsolicited manuscripts is less than 20%. *Survival* does not normally provide referees' comments in the event of rejection. Authors are permitted to submit simultaneously elsewhere so long as this is consistent with the policy of the other publication and the Editors of *Survival* are informed of the dual submission.

Readers are encouraged to comment on articles from the previous issue. Letters should be concise, no longer than 750 words and relate directly to the argument or points made in the original article.

Survival: Global Politics and Strategy (Print ISSN 0039-6338, Online ISSN 1468-2699) is published bimonthly for a total of 6 issues per year by Taylor & Francis Group, 4 Park Square, Milton Park, Abingdon, Oxon, OX14 4RN, UK. Periodicals postage paid (Permit no. 13095) at Brooklyn, NY 11256.

Airfreight and mailing in the USA by agent named World Container Inc., c/o BBT 150-15, 183rd Street, Jamaica, NY 11413, USA.

US Postmaster: Send address changes to Survival, World Container Inc., c/o BBT 150-15, 183rd Street, Jamaica, NY 11413, USA.

Subscription records are maintained at Taylor & Francis Group, 4 Park Square, Milton Park, Abingdon, OX14 4RN, UK.

Subscription information: For more information and subscription rates, please see tandfonline.com/pricing/journal/TSUR. Taylor & Francis journals are available in a range of different packages, designed to suit every library's needs and budget. This journal is available for institutional subscriptions with online-only or print & online options. This journal may also be available as part of our libraries, subject collections or archives. For more information on our sales packages, please visit librarianresources.taylorandfrancis.com.

For support with any institutional subscription, please visit help.tandonline.com or email our dedicated team at subscriptions@tandf.co.uk.

Subscriptions purchased at the personal rate are strictly for personal, non-commercial use only. The reselling of personal subscriptions is prohibited. Personal subscriptions must be purchased with a personal cheque, credit card or BAC/wire transfer. Proof of personal status may be requested.

Back issues: Taylor & Francis Group retains a current and one-year back-issue stock of journals. Older volumes are held by our official stockists to whom all orders and enquiries should be addressed: Periodicals Service Company, 351 Fairview Avenue, Suite 300, Hudson, NY 12534, USA. Tel: +1 518 537 4700; email psc@periodicals.com.

Ordering information: To subscribe to the journal, please contact T&F Customer Services, Informa UK Ltd, Sheepen Place, Colchester, Essex, CO3 3LP, UK. Tel: +44 (0) 20 8052 2030; email subscriptions@tandf.co.uk.

Taylor & Francis journals are priced in USD, GBP and EUR (as well as AUD and CAD for a limited number of journals). All subscriptions are charged depending on where the end customer is based. If you are unsure which rate applies to you, please contact Customer Services. All subscriptions are payable in advance and all rates include postage. We are required to charge applicable VAT/GST on all print and online combination subscriptions, in addition to our online-only journals. Subscriptions are entered on an annual basis, i.e., January to December. Payment may be made by sterling cheque, dollar cheque, euro cheque, international money order, National Giro or credit cards (Amex, Visa and Mastercard).

Disclaimer: The International Institute for Strategic Studies (IISS) and our publisher Informa UK Limited, trading as Taylor & Francis Group ('T&F'), make every effort to ensure the accuracy of all the information (the 'Content') contained in our publications. However, IISS and our publisher T&F, our agents and our licensors make no representations or warranties whatsoever as to the accuracy, completeness or suitability for any purpose of the Content. Any opinions and views expressed in this publication are the opinions and views of the authors, and are not the views of or endorsed by IISS or our publisher T&F. The accuracy of the Content should not be relied upon and should be independently verified with primary sources of information, and any reliance on the Content is at your own risk. IISS and our publisher T&F make no representations, warranties or guarantees, whether express or implied, that the Content is accurate, complete or up to date. IISS and our publisher T&F shall not be liable for any losses, actions, claims, proceedings, demands, costs, expenses, damages and other liabilities whatsoever or howsoever caused arising directly or indirectly in connection with, in relation to or arising out of the use of the Content. Full Terms & Conditions of access and use can be found at http://www.tandfonline.com/page/terms-and-conditions.

Informa UK Limited, trading as Taylor & Francis Group, grants authorisation for individuals to photocopy copyright material for private research use, on the sole basis that requests for such use are referred directly to the requestor's local Reproduction Rights Organization (RRO). The copyright fee is exclusive of any charge or fee levied. In order to contact your local RRO, please contact International Federation of Reproduction Rights Organizations (IFRRO), rue du Prince Royal, 87, B-1050 Brussels, Belgium; email ifrro@skynet.be; Copyright Clearance Center Inc., 222 Rosewood Drive, Danvers, MA 01923, USA; email info@copyright.com; or Copyright Licensing Agency, 90 Tottenham Court Road, London, W1P 0LP, UK; email cla@cla.co.uk. This authorisation does not extend to any other kind of copying, by any means, in any form, for any purpose other than private research use.

Submission information: See https://www.tandfonline.com/journals/tsur20

Advertising: See https://taylorandfrancis.com/contact/advertising/

Permissions: See help.tandfonline.com/Librarian/s/article/Permissions

All Taylor & Francis Group journals are printed on paper from renewable sources by accredited partners.

February–March 2023

Towards Nuclear Stewardship with China

Hans Binnendijk and David C. Gompert

With the rising risk of complex crises and military escalation in the Pacific region, the United States should invite China into a process of nuclear restraint and confidence-building, which we call 'nuclear stewardship'. This process could start with a joint bilateral declaration that neither superpower would use nuclear weapons first against the other or its formal allies. This would acknowledge that neither side could gain by striking first with a nuclear device. This declaration could be the leading edge of a broader set of discussions on strategic stability and eventual implementation of confidence-building measures designed to enhance mutual understanding and trust in the US–Chinese nuclear relationship.

While some might argue that a no-first-use (NFU) pledge is flawed because it could be ignored in a crisis, it would nonetheless help start a process aimed at reducing mutual suspicion about the nuclear motives of the other party. And such a pledge could be reinforced in peacetime by monitoring the military exercises of the other party and in a crisis by America's overwhelming nuclear strength. The benefits far outweigh the risks.

Such an initiative would introduce a cooperative pursuit in an otherwise fraught relationship, while also setting an example for other nuclear-weapons states. Conventional deterrence in the region can be sustained

Hans Binnendijk is a distinguished fellow at the Atlantic Council. He previously served as senior director for defense policy at the US National Security Council, principal deputy director of the US State Department's Policy Planning Staff, and director of the US Institute for National Strategic Studies. He was editor of *Survival* from 1988 to 1991. **David C. Gompert** is a distinguished visiting professor at the US Naval Academy. He previously served as the acting director of national intelligence, special assistant to the US president, deputy under secretary of state, and vice president of the RAND Corporation.

Survival | vol. 65 no. 1 | February–March 2023 | pp. 7–20   https://doi.org/10.1080/00396338.2023.2172846

with strong US and allied defence efforts, and Asian allies can be further reassured that the US will defend them conventionally and deter nuclear strikes on their territory. The US declaration would not apply to Russia, North Korea or Iran (should that nation cross the nuclear threshold). The timing for this initiative is propitious.

Dangerous times

Tension between the United States and China has been growing steadily. This stems from conflicting Chinese and American goals. Now that it is powerful, China seeks to recover territory it feels was taken when it was weak and, more than that, to be the leading power in the Pacific region. It views the United States – its military presence, alliances and influence – as its main obstacle. For its part, the United States has its own interests to protect, including defending its allies and upholding the freedom of the seas. It will not – arguably, cannot – cede this vital region to Chinese dominance.

Within this geopolitical face-off, particular problems take on great danger of spiralling into conflict. The most salient of these is China's intention to expedite unification with Taiwan.[1] China believes the United States' 'One China' policy is eroding and it is becoming impatient for reunification. This sensitivity explains China's militarised response to Nancy Pelosi's visit to Taiwan as speaker of the US House of Representatives in 2022, as well as its increasingly frequent and blatant displays of military might. Tensions also extend to the disputes over sovereign claims in the South and East China seas, affecting US allies including Japan and the Philippines, and new friends such as Vietnam. Given China's heightened aggressiveness, the United Kingdom and Australia have joined the United States in the AUKUS military arrangement that shares defence technologies and strengthens deterrence. Similarly, Australia, India, Japan and the United States re-established in 2017 a Quadrilateral Security Dialogue which includes defence cooperation and invites other Asian partners to participate. Both deepen Chinese fears of US-orchestrated encirclement. Japan is embarking on a major defence build-up and has made clear it will act along with the United States to secure the region at large.

Regional tensions have been amplified by China's military modernisation. According to US Defense Secretary Lloyd J. Austin III, China is now the 'pacing threat' for US worldwide force planning.[2] Although China's annual defence budget is about one-third of America's – roughly $287 billion compared to about $759bn for America in 2022[3] – it is almost entirely spent on Pacific capabilities, whereas the United States has global security interests and demands. The Chinese are directing new investment towards expanding, extending the range and improving the accuracy of its missiles, as well as towards intelligence, surveillance and reconnaissance (ISR) systems, including space and counter-space capabilities. The Chinese navy has invested heavily in diesel attack submarines, frigates and corvettes, and it now outnumbers the US Navy in terms of overall platforms. These efforts are intended to create a conventional advantage for China within the First Island Chain. The United States is responding deliberately with plans for a more dispersed and elusive force, emphasising submarines, uninhabited vessels and drone aircraft, to be integrated in a space-based Joint All-Domain Command and Control System. While neither power wants armed conflict, the dynamics of this military rivalry is increasing the likelihood and potential severity of crises.

In November 2021, presidents Joe Biden and Xi Jinping discussed holding strategic-stability talks to reduce these risks, but the effort stalled.[4] A year later, during a meeting on 14 November in Bali, the two presidents again sought to defuse the tension. They noted the importance of managing their competition carefully and avoiding open conflict. They agreed to keep lines of communication open and to establish working groups to discuss differences, as well as to advance cooperation where possible, such as on climate change, global macroeconomic stability, health security and global food security.[5]

In Bali, the two presidents reiterated their belief that a nuclear war can never be won and must not be fought, and they made known their opposition to the threatened use of nuclear weapons by Russia in Ukraine. This particular convergence of views offers a glimmer of hope that the US and China could partner to lead in fostering nuclear stewardship by embracing the responsibility to govern these uncommonly dangerous weapons with uncommon restraint and to encourage other nuclear-weapons states to show similar restraint. But the two stopped short of creating an agenda to pursue these ideas for greater nuclear stability. American officialdom is preoccupied with the question of how to deal with the projected growth of China's nuclear arsenal. The moment for traditional arms-control negotiations aimed at capping numbers of nuclear weapons has not yet come, as China has thus far rejected negotiations that would codify the overwhelming American and Russian quantitative lead.

More fundamentally, it needs to be asked whether numerical limits are the best way, at the outset, to engender nuclear stability with China. After all, the ultimate goal of arms control is to lessen the danger of nuclear war. The initial US goals should be to prevent military escalation from going nuclear, to diminish the role of nuclear weapons in Pacific security, and to lay a foundation for nuclear stewardship, led by the world's two superpowers.

The alternative we propose is to start by squarely addressing the danger of nuclear instability by instituting a set of stability measures. This could begin with a Sino-US bilateral and reciprocal nuclear NFU declaration. But it must not end with that. The two superpowers could collaboratively craft confidence-building measures to reinforce NFU, expand transparency, avert misunderstandings and avoid actions that could ignite a nuclear war. Throughout this process, the two sides' concepts, intentions and vocabulary concerning nuclear weapons could be clarified in an effort to strive for greater understanding, and with it greater nuclear stability.

Layers of instability in Sino–US security relations

At the heart of the rationale for agreed Sino-American restraint in the use of nuclear weapons is the need to prevent regional geopolitical and military instabilities from escalating to nuclear war. While neither power has any desire to wage nuclear war, instabilities can alter assessments, spawn miscalculations and accentuate fears that could lead to fateful choices. There is a particular danger of this happening in relation to three types of instability in the Pacific:

Festering sovereignty disputes. Contending sovereignty claims, often involving territory or resources, are historically a major cause of war. Chinese claims to sovereignty over Taiwan and within the 'nine-dash line' of the South China Sea put China in potential conflict with the United States and its partners in Asia. China has traditionally not ruled out the use of force to unite with Taiwan, but more recently the patience of Chinese leaders, especially Xi, seems to have worn thin. The Chinese believe that the US is retreating from the One China policy. Some American observers believe that China will try forcefully to unite with Taiwan during Xi's current term of office.

A US-led diplomatic initiative might reduce this festering dispute by gaining agreement from China not to invade Taiwan in exchange for a clear Taiwanese pledge not to declare independence. The United States would, as part of such a diplomatic package, formally reinforce its One China policy and note that its hardening defence commitments to Taiwan are contingent upon Taiwan's restraint with regard to an independence claim. This initiative might need adjustment or even fail, but would at the very least test China's intent.

Crisis instability. Should instability over sovereignty claims cause a crisis, existing conventional military technology could propel the parties from confrontation towards hostilities. With the advent of advanced information systems, a 'targeting revolution' has given both sides the ability to locate and track the other's forces with precision at great and growing distances, and to deliver precision weapons, mainly missiles, at those distances. Consequently, the conventional-strike capabilities of each side are increasingly vulnerable to the strike capabilities of the other. This rewards the side that strikes first and penalises restraint. In a crisis, the logic of how to avoid a war could be displaced by the logic of how to avoid losing a war. These dynamics are somewhat akin to the Schlieffen Plan in 1914, which seemed to reward rapid German action and penalise delay.

China and the United States are racing to master a new generation of 'deep' technologies, among them artificial intelligence (AI), quantum computing and complex autonomous systems. Used to enhance military systems, these could contribute to crisis instability. AI gives machines the power to make choices based on abundant data, which raises the possibility of decisions that are more hostile and less inhibited than those under the control of human beings. Quantum computing will accelerate the processing of data and present leaders with far more information at faster speeds than is the case now; indeed, the goal is to accelerate decision-making. In addition, commanders might be more inclined to use uncrewed platforms (with little danger of loss of life) rather than crewed ones, but in ways that can start a war that kills human beings. Notwithstanding such hazards, neither side will hesitate to develop and use these technologies.

Escalation instability. Should a war with China begin, it could escalate rapidly.[6] The advantage of using rather than withholding strike systems would be increasingly pronounced after hostilities begin. Hesitation could lead to defeat. Sino-American armed conflict could become very destructive very quickly, and difficult to control or end. For instance, China would likely attack American targets, such as aircraft carriers and air bases, from mainland sites. The United States could not allow a Chinese sanctuary from which to attack US forces, and so would conduct strikes on China proper. 'Kill the kill chain' is a term of art in US warfare.

This is where the likelihood of using nuclear weapons could rise sharply. Although China has not adopted the Russian doctrine that attacks on the homeland would merit a nuclear response, the Chinese could interpret American conventional attacks as a prelude to an attempt to disarm China's nuclear capability. Such a perception, even if mistaken, could be amplified if US kinetic or cyber targets included leadership nodes or nuclear command-and-control networks. Or, the United States might target Chinese missile-launch infrastructure, given the lethality and reach of Chinese conventional missiles. With its relatively immature early-warning ISR system, China might misread US intentions and launch nuclear weapons on warning lest they be destroyed. It cannot be excluded that the United States will mistake Chinese preparations to launch non-nuclear weapons as preparations for nuclear ones, and so strike first.

In cases like these, when conventional war reaches the outskirts of nuclear war, the danger of the latter can rise steeply. This is why NFU is important but not sufficient. While the credibility of reciprocal NFU pledges could plummet under such circumstances, accompanying confidence-building measures could lessen the dangers of mistakes and excessive suspicion.

Chinese nuclear posture

The Chinese have long embraced the standard of 'minimal deterrence' in sizing their nuclear arsenal. In essence, this standard requires China to maintain whatever forces it must – no more, no less – to pose a credible threat of devastating retaliation. This implies that strategic delivery systems be sufficiently destructive, survivable and capable of penetrating defences to assure a robust second strike.

The Chinese are increasing the aggregate number, diversity and survivability of their arsenal. They are moving to less vulnerable mobile and solid-fuel delivery systems. China currently has some 100 intercontinental ballistic missiles (ICBMs) and 48 submarine-launched ballistic missiles (each with a single warhead), which together constitute the core of its strategic deterrent capability vis-à-vis the United States, as well as Russia. It is developing new mobile and more accurate DF-31B and DF-41 solid-fuel missiles capable of carrying multiple warheads and of striking US territory. Within the region, China has deployed some 150 intermediate-range nuclear missiles, and is developing both a new DF-17 medium-range missile and CJ-100 cruise missiles. That is a total of some 350–400 Chinese nuclear warheads now deployed.[7] The United States does not normally deploy non-strategic nuclear weapons in the region.

The Pentagon's 2022 'China Military Power Report' estimates that China could deploy a total of 1,000 nuclear warheads by 2030 and 1,500 by 2035. The report notes that work continues on three new, large Chinese ICBM fields, and that last year, China fielded its first long-range nuclear-capable bomber.[8]

China's current nuclear force is consistent with its declared policy of minimal deterrence and NFU. Even the modest force of 100–150 deliverable intercontinental warheads is more than adequate to deter an American first nuclear strike, whether the US admits that or not. At the same time, the current Chinese force posture does not create a first-strike threat against the United States, which should be seen as stabilising by both sides.

Why then is China growing its nuclear force structure beyond what it has for years considered to be optimal? There are several possible explanations:

- China feels that higher warhead levels are needed to sustain minimal deterrence because of growing US prompt-global-strike capabilities, potential anti-ballistic-missile capabilities and cyber-strike technologies that could disrupt command and control;
- China does not want to adopt a dangerous launch-on-warning policy, so it requires a larger retaliatory force to ride out any first strike;

- China wants to break out of its minimal deterrent posture and achieve greater parity with the United States to demonstrate that it is a true superpower;
- China wants a large enough nuclear force so that it can pursue its sovereign ambitions in Taiwan and in the South and East China seas without American interference; and/or
- China wants enough nuclear weapons to deter what it sees as an erratic Russia.

Gaining greater insight into China's rationale for a larger nuclear force should be a principal goal of the strategic-stability dialogue recommended here. If the reasons relate to maintaining minimal deterrence or avoiding a launch-on-warning posture, then confidence-building measures could be designed to alleviate Chinese concerns. If the motive appears to be creating opportunities for conventional operations against Taiwan, additional US conventional-deterrent measures may be needed. If the motive is more diplomatic, such as gaining a higher degree of parity with the US to demonstrate superpower status, then alternative political approaches might be designed.

America's nuclear posture

The US National Defense Strategy declares that the most comprehensive and serious challenge to US national security is China's coercive and increasingly aggressive behaviour.[9] This is mainly because of Chinese enhancements in targeting and conventional strike within the vital Pacific region. Though expanding, China's small nuclear-missile force does not now feature in the configuration of US nuclear forces. Rather, the size and qualities of the United States' nuclear posture are currently geared almost entirely to Russian nuclear forces, as shaped and constrained by arms-control agreements.

The US Nuclear Posture Review (NPR), released in October 2022 together with the National Defense Strategy, notes that although the fundamental role of US nuclear weapons is to deter nuclear attack, they may also deter all forms of strategic attack, assure allies and partners, and allow the US to achieve its objectives if deterrence fails.[10]

This declaratory policy extends to nuclear use in response to 'high consequence' attacks of a strategic though non-nuclear nature, which could include biological-weapons attacks or debilitating cyber attacks.[11] Though the NPR's bar for nuclear use remains very high, it stops short of the 'sole use' doctrine advocated by Biden during the 2020 presidential campaign and of an NFU declaration.[12] American 'negative security assurances' continue to commit to countries that have signed and abide by the Nuclear Non-Proliferation Treaty that the US will not use nuclear weapons against them.

The NPR emphasises the need for the United States to provide credible nuclear deterrence against attacks on itself and its treaty allies. Admiral Charles Richard, while serving as the commander of US Strategic Command in 2022, noted that his team was 'furiously' rewriting a new nuclear-deterrence theory to account for the need to deter both Russia and China simultaneously.[13] That assessment needs to recognise that each country presents a different nuclear threat, and that different strategies are required.

Plans to upgrade America's nuclear force are substantial. The Congressional Budget Office estimates that the US will spend $634bn during the next ten years for the sustainment and modernisation of its nuclear arsenal.[14] The United States has already refurbished many of its nuclear-delivery systems. Upgrades include a new Ground Based Strategic Deterrent to replace *Minuteman* III; new *Columbia*-class ballistic-missile submarines to replace the *Ohio*-class submarines; the B-21 *Raider* bomber to replace the B-2; and new Long-Range Standoff Weapons.[15] These formidable upgrades are more than adequate to offset new Russian strategic-missile developments and growth in China's inventory. At the same time, they should not pose an additional nuclear threat to China.

With such formidable nuclear forces and superiority in conventional forces, it is fair to question whether the United States' nuclear capabilities are needed as insurance against conventional military defeat, as opposed to deterring nuclear attack by confronting nuclear-armed adversaries with the certainty of devastating retaliation.

Developing nuclear stewardship with China

The NPR placed no emphasis on entering a 'strategic dialogue' with China, which we consider essential to enhancing nuclear stability in the vital and precarious Pacific region. Such a dialogue might be initiated by an offer to

China to enter into a bilateral NFU agreement with three conditions. Firstly, the Chinese would acknowledge that such an agreement would cover US allies; logically, this should not give China cause to object, because it already pledges NFU globally. Secondly, the Chinese would agree to enter into a process to foster transparency and to build confidence in support of an NFU agreement, and nuclear stability more generally. Thirdly, China would agree to work with the United States to strengthen nuclear steward-ship globally, which might include constraining Russian and North Korean nuclear belligerence – actions which are in China's interest.

Compatible with a bilateral NFU pledge would be a mutual understand-ing that both sides are *already* highly vulnerable to the nuclear weapons of the other side. Thus far, the United States has resisted such an understand-ing. This would be an important element of any dialogue and could serve to limit China's desire for a massive build-up.[16]

Such talks should engender improved understanding of the dynamics of crisis and escalation instability, and thus reinforce the need to decouple nuclear weapons from such risks. Confidence-building measures should include crisis-management protocols, effective and tested hotlines for inci-dent management, and talks aimed at gaining a clearer and ultimately converging understanding of why each power has the nuclear forces it does. In due course, other nuclear confidence-building measures worth consider-ing could include agreement not to interfere with each other's early-warning and nuclear command-and-control mechanisms, both of which could be highly destabilising; pre-launch warnings and shared early-warning agree-ments similar to those being negotiated with the Russians at the end of the Clinton administration; transparency measures to alert each side to future nuclear-modernisation efforts and to provide explanations for them; and mutual on-site inspections where helpful.

Towards the end of this strategic dialogue augmented by confidence-building measures, mutual limits might be agreed on deployed warheads held by the US and China. Such a goal would flow logically from greater strategic understanding, as it did with the Soviet Union during the Cold War. If China comes to understand that its minimal deterrent posture can be achieved, perhaps at a higher level, but without achieving parity with the US, then progress in achieving agreements similar to the Strategic Arms Reduction Treaty might be made. But given Russia's aggressive nuclear doctrine, trilateral strategic arms-control limitations seem implausible and unwise. The United States will need to achieve one deterrence arrangement with an aggressive Russia that is used to nuclear parity, and another with a China that may still be searching for a new form of minimal deterrence.

The concept of nuclear stewardship should extend to joint efforts to lessen nuclear instability across the region. To this end, the two super-powers should affirm their commitment to denuclearisation of the Korean Peninsula. Meanwhile, the United States must bolster nuclear deterrence there, while keeping China abreast of its intentions as part of the process of confidence-building.

Ensuring the security of American allies

In contemplating a strategic initiative to lessen the danger of nuclear war in the Pacific, the United States should seek the full-throated endorsement of its allies. To achieve this, it must approach them with a compelling case before any approach is made to Beijing. That case rests on two beliefs: that instability in the Pacific region must not result in nuclear war; and that the United States and its allies should and can rely on non-nuclear military means to thwart Chinese aggression. This includes both conventional forces and cyber capabilities, in which the United States is superior.

Among US treaty allies in the region, only South Korea and Japan would have the most immediate concerns. South Korea will want to be sure that American adherence to Sino-US NFU would not prevent the United States from using whatever means necessary to defend against North Korean aggression. A US NFU pledge should not apply to North Korea. It cannot be ruled out that North Korea would threaten a nuclear attack on South Korea, Japan or the United States. Given the scale and locations of North Korea's nuclear weapons, the United States cannot be sure that these could be destroyed in their entirety with conventional strikes. Therefore, the United States cannot foreclose the limited use of nuclear weapons to prevent a North Korean nuclear attack. The NFU agreement with China proposed here would not preclude such an action.

Some Japanese defence officials may be concerned that a US–Chinese NFU pledge would weaken America's defence commitment to Tokyo. That concern can be dealt with by constantly strengthening US and allied militaries, and by demonstrating America's ability to reinforce quickly and sustain conventional conflict in the region if need be. When combined with US conventional forces, Japan's plans to improve its defence forces – including by extending their range – will ensure superiority over any Chinese conventional force threatening Japan for the indefinite future. Washington should provide Tokyo with its full support in assisting and integrating Japan's growing military strength. Given its history, Japan should in general be supportive of an initiative to reduce the danger of nuclear war.

At the same time – and fully consistent with the Sino-US nuclear-stability initiative proposed here – the United States should take additional steps to reassure its Asian allies that the US will continue to deter both conventional and nuclear attacks against them. For example, because Japan and Australia are core members of the US-led alliances meant to deter China, these particular allies could be invited to participate in trilateral nuclear-policy talks, akin to NATO's Nuclear Planning Group. Similar arrangements could be made for South Korea.

The defence of Taiwan provides perhaps the greatest challenge given China's growing military reach across the Taiwan Strait. President Biden has now on four occasions stated publicly that the United States would send troops to defend Taiwan in keeping with the Taiwan Relations Act, which states that 'any effort to determine the future of Taiwan by other than peaceful means, including by boycotts or embargoes' would be considered 'a threat to the peace and security of the Western Pacific area and of grave concern to the United States'.[17] The US Congress has recently passed $2bn in new arms-transfer loans to further strengthen Taiwan's defensive posture. Japan has also indicated that it would help defend Taiwan. Beijing has witnessed the global opposition to Russia's actions in Ukraine and the difficulties Russia has had in occupying even parts of Ukraine, without having the Taiwan Strait or US troops to contend with. Russian territory has served as a sanctuary for Moscow in the Ukraine war. Chinese territory would probably not be a sanctuary in a war with the United States. Short of an outright and foolish Taiwanese declaration of independence, Beijing should be deterred from attacking Taiwan by the prospect of conventional war with the United States and Japan.

Meanwhile, America's NATO allies will be seized with consideration of the implications for the Alliance of a Sino-US nuclear understanding. While they would surely see the advantages of such an understanding for the Pacific, they will be sensitive to indications that the United States has similar intentions towards Russia. Although NATO has overwhelming conventional military superiority over Russia, attempting to draw Russia into an NFU pledge would be fruitless. Because its conventional capabilities are poor and declining, Russia depends on the threat of using nuclear weapons should its territory be attacked. The United States should advise NATO allies that it has no intention of raising NFU in Europe despite its conventional military superiority.

*   *   *

The proposal for a US–Chinese reciprocal nuclear NFU declaration is made as an opening gambit in a longer process to achieve greater nuclear stability in Asia, and thus to reduce the risk of nuclear war. Structured the right way, it is certainly not a concession to China. Nor is it a panacea. It would apply only to China. Such a joint declaration may be difficult to monitor or rely on during an escalation crisis, but it could create enough confidence to begin a process that might produce other positive military and diplomatic outcomes. There is enough commonality of interests to make the effort. If this proposal fails to stabilise US–Chinese nuclear relations, it is reversible.

Notes

[1] See 'Blinken Says China Rejects Status Quo of Taiwan Situation', Reuters, 26 October 2022.

[2] US Department of Defense, '2022 National Defense Strategy of the United States of America', 27 October 2022, p. iii.

[3] On the Chinese budget, see Jon Grevatt and Andrew MacDonald, 'China Increases 2022 Defense Budget by 7.1%', *Janes*, 7 March 2022. Using purchasing power parity, the Chinese defence budget is closer to $350bn – see Peter Robertson, 'Debating Defense Budgets: Why Military Purchasing Power Parity

Matters', VOX CERP, 9 October 2021, table 1. On the US budget, see Earl Timothy, 'U.S. Defense Budget 2022', ExecutiveGov, 27 June 2022.

4 See Naoko Aoki, 'First Steps for Possible U.S.–China Strategic Stability Talks', *Georgetown Journal of International Affairs*, 8 February 2022.

5 White House, 'Readout of President Joe Biden's Meeting with President Xi Jinping of the People's Republic of China', 14 November 2022.

6 See David Gompert, Astrid Cevallos and Christina Garafola, *War with China: Thinking Through the Unthinkable* (Santa Monica, CA: RAND Corporation, 2016).

7 Hans Binnendijk, 'Deterring Nuclear Threats from China', Atlantic Council, November 2021.

8 US Department of Defense, 'Military and Security Developments Involving the People's Republic of China 2022', 29 November 2022, pp. ix, 97.

9 US Department of Defense, '2022 National Defense Strategy of the United States of America', p. 4.

10 US Department of Defense, '2022 Nuclear Posture Review', 27 October 2022, p. 7.

11 Hans Kristensen and Matt Korda, 'The 2022 Nuclear Posture Review: Arms Control Subdued by Military Rivalry', Federation of American Scientists, 27 October 2022.

12 'Sole purpose' differs from an NFU in that it is vaguer and not a firm *ex ante* constraint. Sole purpose would indicate that nuclear weapons are weapons of extreme last resort, grammar notwithstanding. See Ankit Panda and Vipin Narang, 'Sole Purpose Is Not No First Use: Nuclear Weapons and Declaratory Policy', *War on the Rocks*, 22 February 2021, https://warontherocks.com/2021/02/sole-purpose-is-not-no-first-use-nuclear-weapons-and-declaratory-policy/.

13 Tara Copp, 'US Military "Furiously" Rewriting Nuclear Deterrence to Address Russia and China, STRATCOM Chief Says', *Defense One*, 11 August 2022.

14 See Arms Control Association, 'US Nuclear Modernization Programs', January 2022, https://www.armscontrol.org/factsheets/USNuclearModernization.

15 Two nuclear systems were dropped in the NPR: the nuclear sea-launched cruise missile (which was seen as expensive and redundant) and the B83-1 bomb.

16 For elaboration of this concept, see George Perkovich, 'Engaging China on Strategic Stability and Mutual Vulnerability', Carnegie Endowment for International Peace, 12 October 2022.

17 US Congress, 'H.R.2479 – Taiwan Relations Act', 96th Congress (1979–1980), https://www.congress.gov/bill/96th-congress/house-bill/2479.

Rethinking Arms Control with a Nuclear North Korea

Toby Dalton and Jina Kim

North Korea has possessed nuclear weapons for more than a decade. It has conducted as many nuclear-explosive tests as India and Pakistan, and probably retains an arsenal numbering some 20–30 warheads.[1] It fields an array of missiles that can carry nuclear weapons to points as far as Washington DC and as close as metropolitan Seoul. North Korean leader Kim Jong-un has described nuclear weapons as a 'powerful treasured sword'.[2] The probability that he will voluntarily negotiate the denuclearisation of his arsenal in the near future is vanishingly small, perhaps comparable to the odds of global nuclear disarmament or North Korea's chances of winning the 2026 World Cup.

The declared policies of the United States, South Korea, Japan and others toward North Korea seem not to have grasped this. These states continue to espouse a policy of complete denuclearisation while sustaining severe economic sanctions on North Korea, despite the clear lack of tangible, positive results from this approach. No leader wants to acknowledge policy failure, but the costs and risks of continuing to pursue denuclearisation as the paramount objective toward North Korea are rising with the growth of Pyongyang's nuclear arsenal, its development of tactical nuclear weapons and its adoption of a nuclear war-fighting strategy.[3] Since North Korea will not disarm voluntarily,

Toby Dalton is senior fellow and co-director of the Nuclear Policy Program at the Carnegie Endowment for International Peace in Washington DC. **Jina Kim** is Dean of the Division of Language and Diplomacy at Hankuk University of Foreign Studies in Seoul. Previously, she was Chief of the North Korean Military Division at the Korea Institute for Defense Analyses (KIDA).

Survival | vol. 65 no. 1 | February–March 2023 | pp. 21–48   https://doi.org/10.1080/00396338.2023.2172847

the United States and its East Asian allies need to adjust their policies based on an acceptance of the fact that North Korea possesses nuclear weapons.

The obvious and most realistic way of dealing with North Korea's nuclear threat is through deterrence, something that scholars and independent analysts have been advocating for years. Scott Sagan, for instance, argued in September 2017 that 'North Korea no longer poses a non-proliferation problem; it poses a nuclear deterrence problem. The gravest danger now is that North Korea, South Korea, and the United States will stumble into a catastrophic war that none of them wants.'[4] Sagan believes that avoiding war through deterrence requires an end to pre-emptive regime-change threats linked to denuclearisation, and that Kim must instead be convinced that 'the United States will not attempt to overthrow his regime unless he begins a war'. Shifting from denuclearisation to deterrence may seem impolitic to the extent that it tacitly acknowledges North Korea as a nuclear possessor, yet there are few alternatives for dealing with a nuclear-armed adversary.

Deterrence is not a comprehensive strategy for avoiding nuclear Armageddon, however. Indeed, because deterrence is connected with an adversary's capabilities and intentions, states perpetually seek to improve and modernise armaments in ways that can produce arms races and security spirals; they also tend to adopt strategies that prioritise offensive or pre-emptive actions that increase escalation risks.[5] For those reasons, leaders in successive Republican and Democratic administrations in Washington from the mid-1960s found it wise to pursue complementary measures with their Soviet counterparts to mitigate arms racing and to reduce the potential risks and consequences of deterrence failure.[6] Risk-reduction measures took the form of negotiated agreements and declaratory statements to limit and reduce nuclear arms; to provide transparency on military capabilities to reassure adversaries and avoid surprise; and to create more predictability in the two sides' relations. These risk-reduction agreements became commonly known as 'arms control'.

If leaders in Seoul, Tokyo and Washington arrive at a similar conclusion about the need to both deter North Korea and manage deterrence through risk-reduction efforts, how might such an approach work? How could conventional and nuclear capabilities, including those of the United

States, be linked in a comprehensive arms-control process? Thus far, scholarship on the denuclearisation of North Korea has not addressed the problem in these terms. The American and South Korean literature is replete with discussion of phased denuclearisation, yet rarely considers the US and South Korean side of the bargaining or approaches the problem from an arms-control perspective. The literature on conventional arms control on the Korean Peninsula tends to assume the denuclearisation of North Korea without addressing the connections between the two. The few recent studies on nuclear arms control do not consider the complex conventional–nuclear deterrence situation on the peninsula, or the need to simultaneously address North Korean, South Korean and American military capabilities.

Arms control with North Korea is a controversial idea and beyond the boundaries of acceptable policy in Seoul and Washington. However, the existing approach to North Korea carries with it an increasing risk of miscalculation, potentially resulting in catastrophic conflict. Given these risks, it is well worth analysing alternative approaches, even ones as provocative as arms control. Policymakers may ultimately deem comprehensive arms control impractical or unwise, but it is better to debate that proposition than to stick to failing approaches that have been overtaken by events.

Reframing an evolving problem

The standard Western framing of the North Korea problem centres on non-proliferation and the desire to be rid of North Korea's nuclear weapons, hence the repeated calls for 'complete, verifiable, irreversible denuclearization'.[7] The South Korean discourse is similar, but often considers the problem in the context of achieving a peace regime and, ultimately, the reunification of the Korean Peninsula.[8] Given these motivations, ongoing calls for denuclearisation are understandable in political terms – it is easier to maintain that North Korea will disarm – but result in poor policy options. In particular, this framing ignores how the security environment has evolved on the Korean Peninsula since the early 1990s, failing to take into account the complex deterrence equation involving both nuclear and conventional military capabilities, and the South Korea–US alliance.

North Korea's nuclear programme has steadily advanced since the early 1990s, even during periodic negotiated pauses such as the 1994 Agreed Framework, which delayed some elements of the country's nuclear-weapons development but failed to mature into nuclear reversal. As of mid-2021, estimates indicated that North Korea possessed enough fissile material for 45–55 nuclear warheads.[9] It has tested various short-, medium- and long-range nuclear-capable missiles, including manoeuvring missiles seemingly intended to defeat US and South Korean missile-defence systems. North Korean officials assert that the United States' 'hostile policy' is the main driver of nuclear developments,[10] but they have also periodically signalled concerns about growing South Korean military and economic power. In March 2022, for example, in reference to South Korean plans to use conventional missile-strike capabilities to pre-empt a North Korean nuclear attack, senior North Korean official Pak Jong-chon warned that South Korean military officials 'must be crazy or silly to speak of "preemptive strike" on the nuclear weapons state'.[11] In addition to nuclear capabilities, North Korea is modernising its artillery and multiple-rocket systems to hit military targets in South Korea.

The US, South Korea and North Korea have defaulted to deterrence

To defend against North Korea's burgeoning capabilities, South Korea continues to invest in a suite of upgraded conventional capabilities: F-35 fighter aircraft, attack submarines, and ballistic and cruise missiles to enable a 'kill-chain' pre-emptive counterforce strike to disable North Korean nuclear missiles on the launch pad.[12] The United States and South Korea have taken steps to enhance the combined deterrence of North Korea, for instance by conducting joint military exercises.[13] American nuclear deterrence has been extended to both South Korea and Japan – the so-called 'nuclear umbrella' – under the terms of Washington's bilateral military alliances with each.

With the failure to negotiate a durable denuclearisation agreement or inter-Korean conventional military restraints, the United States, South Korea and North Korea have in most ways defaulted to deterrence to protect their security, even if official policy pronouncements do not reflect this.[14] Increasingly, the parties have worked to generate deterrence effects with both advanced conventional and nuclear weaponry. North Korea uses nuclear and conventional weapons to deter perceived regime-change threats from the US and South Korea. South Korean conventional-strike platforms are aimed at deterring North Korean nuclear coercion. And US extended nuclear deterrence aims to dissuade North Korea from carrying out military attacks against South Korea or nuclear strikes against the United States. Yet, as North Korea's nuclear capabilities have grown, and South Korea and the United States have adapted their capabilities and deterrence posture in response, a security spiral has deepened that has encouraged arms racing and heightened crisis-escalation risks. Unless the parties find an off-ramp from this spiral, subsequent security enhancements by Seoul and Washington will drive Pyongyang to produce ever more nuclear weapons and delivery systems designed to defeat missile defences, and to adapt its nuclear posture to avoid 'use or lose' pressure, which in turn will propel the allies to field additional offensive and defensive capabilities.

Disquieted by the dangers posed by the security spiral and the potential for conflict escalation in an increasingly nuclearised Korean Peninsula, some South Korean and American scholars have begun to consider the potential for nuclear risk reduction or arms control.[15] This framing recognises North Korea's continued possession of nuclear weapons and prescribes successive negotiated restraints on North Korea's nuclear missiles to slow the emerging arms race and to mitigate conflict escalation, as an alternative to pressuring North Korea to agree to the complete, verifiable and irreversible dismantlement of its nuclear enterprise. These studies tend to stop short of considering what North Korea might demand in return, however, such as constraints on South Korean and American military capabilities perceived as threatening in Pyongyang.

The blurring of conventional and nuclear deterrence on the Korean Peninsula suggests that a successful arms-control approach would have to tackle a broad set of military capabilities on each side. Comprehensive arms control would necessarily imply restraints not just on North Korean nuclear weapons, but also on the conventional military capabilities of South Korea and the United States, and perhaps on US nuclear capabilities as well.

Arms control … again?

Pursuing arms control with North Korea is not a new idea. Arguably, the 1994 Agreed Framework featured actions and transparency measures that at the time were considered steps toward ensuring North Korea remained free of nuclear weapons, yet functionally were similar to nuclear-risk-reduction measures. For example, the freeze on plutonium production and monitoring by US experts provided assurance that North Korea's nuclear-weapons capacity remained limited. However, the notion that such steps would constitute nuclear arms control with North Korea was never a consideration at the time. Inter-Korean arms control, on the other hand, has been a much more robust topic of study, with periodic efforts by the two Koreas to translate ideas into practical restraints.

Many scholars believed that serious talks on arms control would follow the signing of a basic accord between the two Koreas and a joint declaration on the denuclearisation of the Korean Peninsula in 1991. With the withdrawal of US forward-deployed nuclear weapons from South Korean territory that year – before North Korea's nuclear ambitions became clear – the two Koreas seemed poised to build a new relationship based on detente, which could enable conventional military restraints despite the continued presence of US military forces in South Korea. One early study, for instance, framed the main objectives for inter-Korean arms control in terms of resolving political and military disputes, and preventing miscalculation and misperception that could escalate into military conflict.[16] This and other contemporary studies downplayed US military capabilities as a relevant factor, assuming instead that the main challenges to inter-Korean arms control would originate in differing priorities and mistrust, a lack of understanding in South Korea of North Korea's anxiety over its continual struggle against the South, and the mishandling of Pyongyang's negotiating tactics.[17] One of the few studies to directly address the role of the United States in inter-Korean arms control considered how and when US military forces could be reduced through negotiations, stipulating that there would be equal ceilings on artillery, tanks and armoured personnel carriers for a combined US–South Korean force and North Korean forces.[18] Otherwise, 'end-state' challenges of this kind tended to be subsumed in broader discussions of security in Northeast Asia that emphasised the need for a regional security mechanism that could address problems arising on the Korean Peninsula, including the continued presence of US military forces in South Korea.[19]

As North Korea's development of nuclear weapons became clear after 1993, giving rise to a perceived need for denuclearisation, the previous logic linking arms control on the Korean Peninsula with wider considerations of regional security gave way to a bifurcated approach in which inter-Korean military issues became subordinate to nuclear discussions between the US and North Korea. In effect, progress toward denuclearisation was seen in South Korea (and probably also in the United States) as a precondition for inter-Korean arms control. If the initial co-evolutionary logic had held, the 1994 Agreed Framework, for example, might have enabled progress on inter-Korean arms control. Following the Agreed Framework, however, when inter-Korean dialogue did occur in parallel with sustained periods of negotiation on nuclear matters, the agenda focused mainly on non-contentious issues, resulting in incremental, rather than comprehensive, steps.[20] This pattern held through the subsequent 2003–09 Six-Party Talks. For instance, at the second inter-Korean summit in October 2007, the two Koreas agreed to hold a defence ministers' meeting in Pyongyang to discuss measures intended to encourage non-aggression and to reduce tensions. Yet the only measure that was successfully implemented was the elimination of propaganda efforts in the Demilitarized Zone (DMZ), which was North Korea's main concern. Other intended measures, such as the notification of military exercises, the exchange of military personnel and the installation of direct military telephone lines, were put on hold and ultimately shelved when nuclear negotiations under the Six-Party Talks stalled.

Notwithstanding the poor record of arms control on the Korean Peninsula to date, the 2018 summits between Moon Jae-in, then president of South Korea, and Kim Jong-un, and between Kim and US president Donald Trump, created new optimism about a breakthrough.[21] The conclusion of the Comprehensive Military Agreement between the two Koreas in September 2018 seemed to indicate that the denuclearisation precondition was weakening, and that inter-Korean arms control could proceed without parallel progress on denuclearisation. In contrast with previous inter-Korean agreements that mostly did not result in the implementation of agreed arms-control steps, the September 2018 military agreement was able to advance beyond initial trust-building to concrete steps to restrain military operations. For the first time, the leaders of the two Koreas defined a shared vision for how to use arms control to achieve mutually agreed objectives, agreeing to substantially reduce the danger of war across the Korean Peninsula and to fundamentally improve their relations.[22] In addition to several operational military constraints, the two Koreas agreed to reduce the risks of accidental or inadvertent provocation and escalation, and to mitigate sources of tension, such as fishing in disputed waters.

The implementation record for the Comprehensive Military Agreement also breaks with past practice. Some of the agreed measures were implemented relatively quickly, and not simply because they were low-cost or logistically easy; destruction of guard posts in the DMZ is a case in point. Several of the implemented measures – such as completing the withdrawal of troops and firearms from 20 front-line guard posts in the DMZ within two months, verifying the demilitarisation work with the UN Command at the Joint Security Area in Panmunjom, and carrying out joint inspections on both sides of the contested border – constituted marked changes in military operations. However, work to implement other measures, such as the establishment of a joint military committee to continue high-level inter-Korean military talks, never started (see Table 1).

Despite the apparent progress made under the 2018 inter-Korean military agreement, events ultimately demonstrated that it remained captive to the prevailing bifurcated negotiating structure, even without being explicitly linked to the nuclear discussions then ongoing between North Korea and the United States. In the absence of any progress in denuclearisation talks, North Korea revealed a new plan for its nuclear posture and increased training exercises, including the firing of hundreds of artillery shells into the maritime buffer zones established by the 2018 Comprehensive Military Agreement, which South Korea criticised as 'overt violations' of the agreement.[23] As in the past, the failure of nuclear negotiations to yield sustained movement toward denuclearisation meant that inter-Korean arms control had limited space to progress. In this sense, the 2018 agreement was also fundamentally disconnected from the evolving security environment on the Korean

Peninsula, and especially from the posturing of strategic military capabilities for deterrence by North Korea, South Korea and the United States.

Toward comprehensive arms control

To overcome the impediments that have frustrated past attempts at inter-Korean arms control, including the denuclearisation precondition, any future arms-control process would need to align with the current strategic environment on the Korean Peninsula. It would need to address both inter-Korean and broader strategic issues not just concurrently, but with some form of cross-linkage – that is to say, in a comprehensive manner. The foundation for this kind of comprehensive approach can be found in the conjoined posturing of both nuclear and conventional military capabilities for deterrence by North Korea, South Korea and the United States. The

Table 1: **Implementation status of measures under the 2018 Comprehensive Military Agreement**

Objective	Measures	Progress
Completely cease all hostile acts against each other in every domain	Suspend artillery training and outdoor-manoeuvre training above the regiment level within five kilometres of the Military Demarcation Line	V
	Install covers on the ports of coastal guns and close the gun gates, and prohibit live-fire artillery drills and maritime-manoeuvre training in agreed waters	P
	Discuss various measures (such as the cessation of reconnaissance and the augmentation of force) to realise phased disarmament	N
Turn the areas around the Northern Limit Line in the West Sea into a maritime peace zone	Establish a peace zone and a joint fishing zone in the West Sea	N
	Plan and develop measures for joint patrol to prevent illegal fishing within the joint fishing zone and to ensure the safety of fishing activities	N
Turn the DMZ into a peaceful area and begin recovery of war remains	Withdraw guard posts that are within 1 km of each other and completely withdraw all guard posts within the DMZ	P
	Demilitarise the Panmunjom Joint Security Area and ensure mutual visits	P
	Jointly plan to excavate war remains within the DMZ	N
Establish a joint military committee and hotlines between military authorities	Continue to discuss the issue of installing and operating a direct line between South and North Korean military authorities	N
	Discuss in detail issues related to the formation and operation of the North–South Joint Military Committee	N
	Jointly check and evaluate the implementation status of military agreements on a regular basis	N
Militarily support cooperation, exchanges, visits and contacts at all levels	Discuss military-security measures for joint use of the Han River estuary	N
	Develop measures for the connection and modernisation of railway roads along the east and west coasts	N
	Discuss the use of direct routes to Haeju and passage through the Jeju Strait through the Joint Military Committee	N

N: Not implemented, P: Partially implemented, V: Implemented but subsequently violated relationship between the nuclear and conventional domains is further indicated by North Korea's threats of attack against South Korea and the United States, and the South Korean–American response in the form of combined conventional military forces and the United States' extended deterrence. More specifically, the growing arsenals of nuclear-capable ballistic and cruise missiles possessed by both South and North Korea, which can carry large conventional or nuclear payloads, blur the physical and conceptual boundaries of conventional and nuclear capabilities. (South Korea does not possess nuclear weapons, but many of its missiles have the technical capacity for nuclear delivery.) South Korea's use of conventional-strike capabilities for strategic deterrence is an important development in this respect.[24]

The blurring of conventional and nuclear forces effectively means that developments in one domain can influence developments in the other. Restraints on nuclear weapons would have implications for conventional military forces, and vice versa. Indeed, the failure of past efforts to restrain North Korea can plausibly be blamed at least in part on the separation of the nuclear and conventional military domains into unlinked negotiating tracks. Managing this complex deterrence dilemma would require risk-reduction measures in both domains. For instance, it may be difficult, perhaps impossible, to devise nuclear-weapons measures that North Korea would agree to in the absence of some reciprocal conventional-military steps by South Korea.

Managing deterrence through comprehensive arms control would also require that some agreed balance of capability be maintained so as to avoid displacing arms races from one domain to the other. Notably, over the past decade, North Korea has carried out a significant modernisation of its conventional forces to make them more suited for limited military operations prosecuted under the threat of nuclear escalation. Its capabilities include hypersonic, manoeuvrable missiles; intelligence, surveillance and reconnaissance (ISR) systems; and armed drones, among others.[25] In addition, North Korea has claimed to be developing tactical nuclear weapons and has threatened to use them early in a conflict.[26] Combined, these capabilities could give North Korea an ability to pursue an asymmetric escalation strategy against South Korea and the United States. A comprehensive arms-control effort could blunt the potential for North Korea to operation-alise this strategy, thus mitigating arms-race risks.

Another consideration for negotiators is that the parties may have wildly different values and priorities in seeking to define and maintain a military balance. Indeed, North Korean leaders may perceive something of a dilemma: restraints in one domain may be acceptable since they could be offset by capabilities in the other, whereas comprehensive restraints would come at greater risk, even though they could result in more reciprocal measures from South Korea and the United States. For example, North Korea might be willing to adopt measures that reduce the threat posed by its long-range artillery and multiple-rocket-launch systems, but only provided that it is able to maintain a sufficient nuclear capability to deter perceived US and South Korean regime-change threats.

A comprehensive negotiation would have to address the dilemmas of arms control for both Koreas. For North Korea, US security guarantees appear to be important, even though North Korean officials have cast doubt on the reliability of such promises and the extent to which they reflect a fundamental change in what they perceive as the United States' hostile policy toward their country.[27] If North Korean leaders feared that a US president might renege on an agreement, they would likely hedge on nuclear and conventional arms control, seeking to retain an ability to reconstitute capabilities. However, linking North Korean nuclear restraints to parallel South Korean and US conventional military restraints might diminish this impulse, thus permitting sustained progress. Similarly, South Korea will be hesitant to constrain or reduce the conventional deterrence capabilities it has been acquiring without corresponding steps by North Korea to restrict both nuclear and conventional capabilities.

A comprehensive approach could address some of the procedural hurdles to past agreement. Explicitly linking nuclear and conventional arms-control negotiations might limit the potential for North Korea to play one track off the other in a bid to maximise concessions, or to try to drive a wedge between South Korea and the United States. That said, an inevitable side effect of linking negotiations across the conventional military and nuclear domains is that a blockage in one track is likely to stymie movement in the other.

Finally, tighter policy planning and coordination between South Korea and the United States would be a necessary condition for negotiating and implementing a comprehensive approach. The inevitable frictions caused by diverging priorities between Seoul and Washington, and fears among South Koreans that US negotiators will not represent their interests, create fissures that North Korea is practised at exploiting. Linking conventional and nuclear issues in ways that implicate both American and South Korean capabilities and force postures would necessitate closer coordination, information-sharing and common negotiating positions.

A comprehensive arms-control typology

A comprehensive negotiation that links conventional- and nuclear-weapons restraints would need to address a range of political, technical and military issues. Studies of past arms-control efforts demonstrate that an excessive focus on technical restraints often leads to failure, while processes that integrate political, military and technical measures tend to have greater durability.[28] With that in mind, a typology is a useful way to organise measures according to characteristics that are applicable across both the nuclear and conventional domains. For a comprehensive arms-control process on the Korean Peninsula, four types of measures are relevant: behavioural, operational, procedural and structural.

Behavioural arms-control steps are principally aimed at creating expectations and predictability about future actions by the parties. This type of measure comprises declaratory actions – whether prescriptive or restrictive – and the associated communications. Prescriptive actions could involve statements of intent to take certain actions, such as pre-notification of military activities. Restrictive measures would involve agreed restraints, such as not making military threats. Behavioural measures could be operationalised through hotlines, periodic meetings among military officers and political officials, or parallel unilateral or joint statements, among other means.

Operational measures are intended to promote predictability by providing buffers against fears of surprise attack and the risks of crisis escalation. Operational restraints could be achieved through restrictions on deployment, posture or exercises, for example by creating force-restriction or exclusion zones near borders, or by proscribing exercises with nuclear forces. More broadly conceived, operational measures can serve to mitigate economic or political sources of tension, for example by facilitating the cooperative administration of territories or resources (such as fisheries or water).

Procedural arms-control measures involve conveying information or providing other forms of transparency to permit the monitoring and verification of commitments. Declarations, reciprocal visits, inspections and overflights are common procedural measures used in arms-control agreements. The value of procedural measures increases when the information or transparency provided is not otherwise easily acquired or monitored; that is, it may be considered a 'costly signal' that gives the adversary a better understanding of a state's military capabilities.[29]

Lastly, structural arms-control measures involve actions that limit the scope and scale of the military capabilities that states are permitted to possess or deploy. Structural measures might take the form of caps, reductions or proscriptions on future developments, whose purpose is to lock in predictability and stability, and to mitigate the impetus for arms racing. Such measures can also increase the costs of rearming. As with operational steps, structural arms control necessitates procedural measures that allow states to affirm that the other side is meeting its obligations. Indeed, monitoring and verification proved to be consistently challenging for the United States and the Soviet Union (later Russia) to negotiate in their arms-reduction talks.

Past inter-Korean conventional arms-control negotiations have primarily employed behavioural and operational measures, interspersed with some procedural steps. Structural measures remain elusive. In the nuclear domain, past negotiations did not embrace arms-control objectives as such (full denuclearisation was the aim, at least for South Korea and the US), yet the Agreed Framework and Six-Party Talks called for measures that could be characterised as behavioural, operational and procedural. Looking ahead to a putative comprehensive negotiation, this typology could help describe how various forms of arms control might be linked across the conventional and nuclear domains.

Organising a comprehensive arms-control negotiation

If North Korea, South Korea and the United States (and perhaps also China and others) agree to comprehensive negotiations on nuclear and conventional military restraints, this will upend the diplomatic structure that has been in place on the Korean Peninsula for the last three decades. The blurring of conventional and nuclear deterrence similarly necessitates breaking down what has been a fairly defined barrier between those domains in past negotiations. Specifically, South Korea would be a party to negotiations on North Korea's nuclear arsenal and the United States would participate in negotiations on conventional arms control, including steps that would affect US Forces Korea. Analytically, the need to consider the particular technical–political issues of each domain makes it useful to retain some separation between them; negotiators might find it easier to apply a similar separation, even as they may seek to pair restraints across domains as a way to reinforce deterrence stability.

Even so, a comprehensive approach argues for adjusting the scope of each domain. Rather than carrying over the 'nuclear' and 'conventional' tracks of old, it would be logical to instead have a 'strategic' and a 'conventional' track. The logic for adopting the 'strategic' nomenclature is to capture a broader range of capabilities possessed by the parties, to include any chemical and biological capabilities rather than just North Korea's nuclear weapons. Specifically, the strategic domain would cover ballistic and cruise missiles capable of carrying a nuclear payload, even if they are deployed in a conventional role. By bringing in dual-capable missiles, the strategic track would engage South Korean and US capabilities, in addition to North Korea's. This is critical, given that both South and North Korea would presumably seek to retain some number of these missiles as conventional weapons. Thus, adopting terminology that creates more equivalence in capabilities between North Korea, South Korea and the US recasts negotiations in ways that might create more space for arms-control diplomacy. Crucially, it would also give South Korea not just a seat at the nuclear table, but also a direct stake in how strategic issues are deemed to intersect with any conventional military restraints.

Table 2 demonstrates how the four-part typology of arms control can be reflected in a negotiation that distinguishes between the conventional and strategic domains, with notional examples of specific steps provided for each. The table outlines a logical way of categorising the various measures, but is agnostic on how they could be combined and sequenced to produce an agreement. Combining and sequencing are primarily political matters, subject to the perceptions of the military balance and what could yield deterrence stability, as well as the typical give and take of negotiations. Understandably, states could be expected to take a cautious approach in their negotiating strategies, including on the desired progression of steps and the risk that one or more parties could defect from the agreement. South Korea and the United States would be especially sensitive to North Korean negotiating gambits aimed at splitting the allies. Negotiators would also be attuned to the risks of hostage-taking during negotiations, in which a state might seek additional concessions in one domain while blocking progress in the other. The need to sustain momentum and to implement a complex agreement could argue for a progression of discrete steps – whether reciprocal in the same domain or across domains. Lastly, negotiations would need to consider whether agreed steps might inadvertently lead to the development of offsetting capabilities or create new escalation risks, especially if negotiations reached the stage of structural restraints.

These considerations suggest two organisational approaches to a comprehensive arms-control negotiation: soft linkage and hard linkage. A soft-linkage approach would effectively enable negotiators to mix and match between different types of arms-control measures to compose agreements across both domains. For example, an initial agreement might include a conventional operational restraint (such as moving artillery 50 kilometres from the DMZ) paired with a strategic procedural step (such as declaring stocks of dual-capable missiles with ranges of up to 1,550 km). In a soft-linkage approach, negotiations could proceed in parallel in the strategic and conventional tracks with less requirement for tight coordination between them, although interim agreements – waypoints – would be necessary to mitigate hostage-taking and purposeful delays in implementation.

In contrast, a hard-linkage approach would bind the negotiations in both domains in more direct ways, by stipulating the agreement of measures within each arms-control type. That is, an interim agreement could

Table 2: **Options for comprehensive arms control**

Type of negotiation	Track	Behavioural measures	Operational measures	Procedural measures	Structural measures
Soft linkage: mixed sequential	Conventional	• New confidence-building measures, such as monitoring of border agreements • Establishment of inter-Korean crisis-management committee • Non-aggression agreement	• Artillery redeployments • Withdrawal of offensive weapons (170/240 mm artillery) • No forward deployment of new weapons (such as North Korea's KN-23 ballistic missile) south of Pyongyang	• Revitalisation of Neutral Nations Supervisory Commission • Notification of brigade-level military exercises	• Disarming of military facilities in the DMZ • Ceiling on active-service personnel (excluding US Forces Korea) • Ceiling on reserve and paramilitary units • Freeze/reduction of rear-area infiltration force • No production of new weapons (such as North Korea's KN-23 and KN-25 ballistic missiles)
	Strategic	• No-first-use and/or sole-purpose declaration (without exceptions such as North Korean nuclear-weapons use against allies of nuclear-weapons states) • Agreement on no nuclear threats • Negative security assurances	• Dual-capable missile de-mating and non-alert agreement (storing launchers, airframes and warheads separately)	• Declarations, fissile-material production freeze and transparency at Yongbyon nuclear facility	• Biological- and chemical-weapons elimination • Destruction of strategic assets • Dual-capable missile-production freeze
Hard linkage: symmetrical and progressive	Conventional	1. North Korea–South Korea military-stability talks	2. Artillery/multiple-rocket-launcher limitation zone	3a. Declaration of artillery pieces/locations within agreed limit 3b. Transparency measures (such as overflights) to confirm artillery exclusion	4a. Ceilings on artillery/multiple-rocket-launcher systems 4b. Change in composition of US Forces Korea
	Strategic	1. US–North Korea nuclear-stability talks	2. Nuclear non-operational deployment agreement and cessation of military exercises involving nuclear forces (or dual-capable missiles) on the Korean Peninsula	3a. North and South Korean declarations of arsenals of dual-capable missiles with ranges up to 1,550 km 3b. Transparency visits to South and North Korean missile-operating bases (potentially also US air or naval bases in theatre)	4a. Ceilings on North and South Korean dual-capable missiles 4b. Ceilings on missile-defence interceptors

comprise reciprocal steps in both the strategic and conventional domains, such as parallel agreements for conventional- and strategic-stability talks. This approach could be similar to the 'action for action' principle used during the Six-Party Talks. In a hard-linkage approach, there would need to be tighter coordination between the negotiations in both tracks, given that there might be synergies to exploit or offsets to avoid.

In either the soft- or hard-linkage approach, progression and sequencing would be key considerations: how to build, step by step, toward structural arms-control measures. In a soft approach, negotiators might adopt the 'one-for-one' principle, necessitating that each interim step comprise one conventional and one strategic measure. The flexibility in this approach may expedite progress, yet could make coordination between domains more difficult. In a hard approach, negotiators might attempt to sequence a series of agreements driven by a prescriptive logic: for instance, from behavioural, to operational, to procedural and finally to structural. A progressive approach like this could reduce flexibility, yet a narrower scope for negotiations might mitigate the potential for hostage-taking. In light of past divergence in North and South Korean approaches to arms-control negotiations, one consideration in a progressive approach is the likelihood of different views about the starting point for negotiations, with North Korea tending to focus on the downgrading of US Forces Korea and South Korea on initial trust-building steps.

Inevitable negotiating challenges

Although a comprehensive arms-control approach to the Korean Peninsula may be better aligned with the current strategic environment, it would still be logistically and politically challenging. The sheer complexity of the effort, not to mention the likelihood of drawn-out negotiations that would span changes of political administration in South Korea and the United States, might doom a comprehensive approach from the outset. Furthermore, US and South Korean domestic politics would likely be thorny, given the implicit legitimacy an arms-control negotiation would give North Korea as a possessor of nuclear weapons. Conservative South Koreans who believe North Korea is attempting to push US forces off the Korean Peninsula and to break up the South Korea–US alliance would be critical of any steps perceived as unequal or unfavourable to South Korean interests. The denuclearisation pre-condition could cast a shadow over the proceedings, given that many South Koreans and Americans would object to any plan under which North Korea was not required to at least promise to completely give up nuclear weapons. Navigating this political landscape would require the South Korean gov-ernment to engage in a two-level game, countering a conservative coalition of politicians and defence scholars at the domestic level while simultane-ously minimising the adverse effects during negotiations with North Korea. Washington also has no shortage of North Korea hawks who would object to any concessions as rewarding North Korea's bad behaviour; they might characterise a process requiring reciprocal restraints by the United States as appeasement. The US administration would also face concerns from Japan that arms-control steps affecting the US military posture in Northeast Asia might diminish the credibility of American defence commitments to Tokyo.

In addition to these notable political challenges, five other challenges would arise during the negotiations themselves. Firstly, perceptions of the military balance among the two Koreas and the United States would be crucial in suc-cessfully linking constraints across the conventional and strategic domains. Diverging perceptions arising from asymmetries of information would make it difficult for the parties to develop a shared understanding of capabilities at the necessary level of granularity. Presumably, North Korean assessments of American and South Korean military strengths are skewed by the coun-try's comparative lack of independent information-gathering capabilities, while North Korea's opacity makes it something of a 'black hole' for US and South Korean intelligence. Any overestimation of the capabilities of each party would make it difficult to identify reciprocal steps that could be agreed to without engendering concerns of vulnerability. Concerns about cheating to preserve certain capabilities or advantages would also be prevalent yet difficult to assuage, especially given the relatively infrequent and episodic interactions between the countries that have precluded the development of common means of resolving disputes arising from information asymmetries.

Not only perceptions but also actual differences in the military balance will pose a further challenge for negotiators to manage. There are broad gulfs

– both quantitative and qualitative – in capability among the parties. These disparities are likely to result in disputes over demands for disproportionate actions. Notably, North Korea has a far larger standing army than South Korea – 1.28 million vs 555,000, according to one estimate[30] – and also enjoys advantages in certain categories of armament. However, obsolescence, a lack of spare parts and basic under-resourcing in North Korea's military suggest that simple quantitative approaches to maintaining a military balance would not be sufficient. Both Koreas are implementing military-modernisation programmes, which means the military balance will be a moving target, and both sides may be reluctant to accept constraints on modernised equipment.

Secondly, there are considerations related to deterrence and the role of weapons systems that have denial or punitive characteristics. Presumably, North Korea would be reluctant to accept operational and structural restraints on its multiple-rocket-launch systems and ballistic missiles, for example, both of which are central to its deterrence-by-punishment strategy. Similarly, South Korea is fielding conventional-strike missiles for pre-emption alongside missile defences, both of which support deterrence by denial. (South Korea also has a punitive leadership-decapitation strategy involving large conventional ordnance.) Whether South Korea and North Korea would be willing to trade reductions in denial capabilities for reductions in punitive capabilities is the type of proposition to be tested in a comprehensive negotiation. If the parties were committed to reducing the potential for conflict escalation and fears of surprise attack, this type of reciprocal constraint could be possible.

Arms control would not necessarily compromise deterrence

Thirdly, reciprocity will be an important element of any agreement. In some instances, reciprocal and equal limits might apply. In others, the limits could be designed to permit some level of asymmetry in similar capabilities or to create a relationship between different types of systems. Proceeding with an arms-control process would not necessarily mean compromising national security or deterrence. Rather, it could be designed to allow the parties to retain sufficient deterrence, particularly in early phases before developing greater confidence in each other not to seek gains by violating agreements. It would be ideal to focus limitations mainly on punitive capabilities to reduce threat levels, but it may be difficult to distinguish clearly between punitive and denial capabilities. For example, South Korea's precision-strike missiles could serve to interdict a North Korean nuclear attack and to execute decapitation operations. Should South Korea retain some of these capabilities for deterrence, this would encourage North Korea to maintain similar capabilities for its own deterrence purposes. Permissible hedging therefore is likely to be a necessary feature of an arms-control framework. To find a balance between maintaining deterrence and sustaining arms control, negotiators could consider various equilibriums of capability that would enable the two Koreas to have confidence in the sufficiency of their forces.

The tit-for-tat arms developments between the two Koreas show how the search for offsets can feed an arms race. For example, North Korea has built a surface-effect ship equipped with a rocket launcher, torpedo tubes and surface-to-air missiles to quickly deliver assault troops to occupy South Korean border islands, as well as very slender vessels capable of carrying special forces to infiltrate South Korean territory.[31] North Korea is also believed to be capable of weaponising some 20 biological and chemical agents such as anthrax, mustard, chlorine, sarin and V-series nerve agents.[32] These are capabilities that do not have obvious analogues in South Korea. In the cyber domain, North Korea can exploit weaknesses in South Korea's defence of its vast digital infrastructure while itself being relatively secure given its limited internet capacity and low level of digitisation. These types of asymmetric capabilities and vulnerabilities may pose distinct challenges to arms control.

Fourthly, although it would be exceedingly difficult to factor asymmetric capabilities into an assessment of military balance, there could be value in agreeing to certain principles, such as non-possession or non-use during peacetime. Eventually, North Korea would need to join the Chemical Weapons Convention and demonstrate compliance with its commitments under the Biological and Toxin Weapons Convention, and accommodate verification procedures. Therefore, North Korea could first declare that it would not possess chemical and biological weapons by a certain date and agree to destroy them in the presence of international observers. These actions could be sequenced with the implementation of a peace regime. Previously, addressing North Korea's chemical- and biological-weapons capability, which poses a clear and demonstrated asymmetric threat to allied forces, was notably missing from both the inter-Korean arms-control discussions and multilateral nuclear negotiations. Many South Koreans were anxious about this missing piece in the arms-control agenda, yet officials clearly feared that efforts to raise such asymmetric capabilities in the talks could discourage North Korea from negotiating on nuclear and conventional restraints, or incentivise the North to demand more quid pro quos. However, if such capabilities are left outside the scope of negotiations, they could develop into a new conflict domain.

The question of how to restructure and modernise their military forces is likely to be a major concern for both Koreas. Recent South Korean defence initiatives aim not only at increasing deterrence capabilities against North Korea's threats, but also at upgrading the nation's overall capabilities to build a more effective military force that can withstand future uncertainties in the region. Force-improvement programmes mandating an average annual defence-budget increase of 7.2% under the 2021–2025 Mid-term Defense Plan are intertwined with the goal of exercising wartime operational control. This goal requires South Korea to have core military capabilities to lead a combined defence force.[33] Some programmes, such as the cyber-threat response system, combat-drone system, reconnaissance-aviation group and naval strategic-manoeuvring capabilities, have multiple purposes. Because not all of Seoul's defence-reform efforts are tied directly to threats from North Korea, trading away newly acquired capabilities as part of an arms-control regime would concern not only South Korea but also the US, which desires South Korea's active participation in broader security efforts in the Indo-Pacific region. Pyongyang is also pursuing military modernisation and, like Seoul, is likely to see its modernised systems as integral to its security in the future, rather than as bargaining chips. Considering the huge sunk costs involved and the two Koreas' stances on military modernisation, it is plausible that both will insist on retaining vital modern weapons systems, which will necessarily hamper the effectiveness of a potential arms-control framework.

Finally, increasing transparency and verifying compliance are essential to the success of any agreements, but have often been a source of disruption in past negotiations with North Korea. In the 1990s, Pyongyang offered several proposals for mutual inspections between the two Koreas, presumably because this would have permitted access not only to South Korean military bases but also to US Forces Korea bases. However, disagreement about reciprocal inspections, especially on the proportionality of inspection sites, scope and the time between advance notice and inspection, led to a stalemate.[34] In the 2000s, North Korea rejected the US-proposed sequencing of nuclear-verification procedures and tried to link verification to other demands, such as a legally binding non-aggression pact with the United States. These ultimately led to the breakdown of the Six-Party Talks in 2008–09.[35]

A framework that links conventional-military and strategic capabilities will require larger numbers and types of sites to be subject to inspection and verification. It would also rely on a far wider array of information that could be gleaned through monitoring and verification. However, a benefit of the linkage approach is that it would formalise opportunities for deal-making across domains and locations. For example, negotiators could discuss a trade of US and South Korean inspections at a North Korean missile-operating base for North Korean inspections at a US Forces Korea base. North Koreans could also be presented with opportunities, such as more autonomous means to monitor developments in the region, so that they could see verification as worth exploring.

*   *   *

Negotiating arms control with North Korea is an idea still well outside the policy consensus in Washington and Seoul, not least because of the 'recognition' issue: some believe that North Korea should not be recognised or accepted as a nuclear-weapons possessor. As one unnamed senior Biden administration official argued, 'There is an extraordinarily strong global consensus ... that [North Korea] should not, and must not, be a nuclear nation. No country is calling for this ... The consequences of changing policy, I think would be profoundly negative.'[36] Yet North Korea possesses dozens of nuclear weapons, and there is strong support for acquiring nuclear weapons in South Korea.[37] It is debatable whether the consequences of policy change could be any worse than those of three decades of failed non-proliferation efforts.

Admittedly, comprehensive arms control may be conceptually plausible but practically impossible. Negotiators would have to thread a very fine needle, especially on reciprocal measures. What could North Korea ask for that would be acceptable to Seoul and Tokyo because it did not weaken US extended deterrence, would not impact Washington's strategic deterrence of China and Russia, and would be politically saleable in Washington? Perhaps it is a null set. But that could only be determined through credible and sustained efforts by the governments to explore the range of possible outcomes.

It is reasonable to expect that North Korea will continue to possess nuclear arms. Short of a devastating war, there are no apparent means of coercing the country to give them up. Therefore, it is worth considering arms control as a policy alternative to denuclearisation. At the very least, pursuing arms control is no more likely to fail than past approaches, and may be beneficial for peace and security in Northeast Asia.

Acknowledgements

This study was supported by the Hankuk University of Foreign Studies Research Fund and a research grant from the Korea National Defense University.

Notes

1   Hans M. Kristensen and Matt Korda, 'North Korean Nuclear Weapons, 2022', *Bulletin of the Atomic Scientists*, vol. 78, no. 5, pp. 273–94, https://doi.org/10.1080/00963402.2022.2109341.

2   Timothy W. Martin and Thomas Grove, 'Kim Jong Un Defends Nuclear Program as North Korea's "Treasured Sword"', *Wall Street Journal*, 8 October 2017, https://www.wsj.com/articles/kim-jong-un-defends-nuclear-program-as-north-koreas-treasured-sword-1507451098.

3   See Ankit Panda, 'North Korea's Dangerous Turn', *Diplomat*, 1 September 2022, https://thediplomat.com/2022/08/north-koreas-dangerous-turn/.

4   Scott D. Sagan, 'The Korean Missile Crisis: Why Deterrence

Is Still the Best Option', *Foreign Affairs*, November/December 2017, https://www.foreignaffairs.com/articles/north-korea/2017-09-10/korean-missile-crisis.

5   See Richard Ned Lebow and Janice Gross Stein, *We All Lost the Cold War* (Princeton, NJ: Princeton University Press, 1995).

6   See Michael Krepon, *Winning and Losing the Nuclear Peace* (Stanford, CA: Stanford University Press, 2021).

7   See, for example, NATO, 'Brussels Summit Communique', 14 June 2021, https://www.nato.int/cps/en/natohq/news_185000.htm?selectedLocale=en.

8   See, for example, Yong-Sup Han, 'Arms Control and Peace on the Korean Peninsula: For a Positive Relationship Between the Two Concepts', *Korea and World Politics*, vol. 22, no. 1, 2006, pp. 167–98.

9   Kristensen and Korda, 'North Korean Nuclear Weapons, 2022'.

10 See, for example, Choe Sang-Hun, 'North Korea Warns Biden Against "Hostile Policy"', *New York Times*, 1 May 2021.

11 Lee Je-hun, 'Kim Yo-jong Upbraids S. Korean Defense Minister, Military over Missile Comments', *Hankyoreh*, 4 April 2022, https://english.hani.co.kr/arti/english_edition/e_north-korea/1037461.html.

12 See Ian Bowers and Henrik Stålhane Hiim, 'Conventional Counterforce Dilemmas: South Korea's Deterrence Strategy and Stability on the Korean Peninsula', *International Security*, vol. 45, no. 3, 2021, pp. 7–39, https://direct.mit.edu/isec/article/45/3/7/95269/Conventional-Counterforce-Dilemmas-South-Korea-s; and

Manseok Lee and Hyeongpil Ham, 'South Korea's Conventional Forces Buildup: The Search for Strategic Stability', *War on the Rocks*, 16 April 2021, https://warontherocks.com/2021/04/south-koreas-conventional-forces-buildup-the-search-for-strategic-stability/.

13 See US Department of Defense, 'Secretary of Defense Lloyd J. Austin III and South Korean Defense Minister Suh Wook Hold a Press Conference Following the 53rd U.S.–Republic of Korea Security Consultative Meeting in Seoul', 2 December 2021, https://www.defense.gov/News/Transcripts/Transcript/Article/2859519/secretary-of-defense-lloyd-j-austin-iii-and-south-korean-defense-minister-suh-w/.

14 Statements from government officials occasionally display an acceptance of deterrence. See, for example, Josh Smith, 'Analysis: US and Allies Turn to Deterring War with North Korea as Options for Preventing Nuclear Tests Dwindle', Reuters, 31 October 2022, https://www.reuters.com/world/us-allies-turn-deterring-war-with-north-korea-options-preventing-nuclear-tests-2022-10-31/.

15 See Jina Kim and John Warden, 'Limiting North Korea's Coercive Nuclear Leverage', *Survival*, vol. 62, no. 1, February–March 2020, pp. 31–8; Toby Dalton and Youngjun Kim, 'Negotiating Nuclear Arms Control with North Korea: Why and How?', *Korean Journal of Defense Analysis*, vol. 33, no. 1, March 2021, https://doi.org/10.22883/kjda.2021.33.1.001; and Ankit Panda, 'The Right Way to Manage a Nuclear North Korea', *Foreign Affairs*, 19 November 2018,

https://www.foreignaffairs.com/articles/north-korea/2018-11-19/right-way-manage-nuclear-north-korea.

16 Yong-Sup Han, 'Designing and Evaluating Conventional Arms Control Measures: The Case of the Korean Peninsula', RAND Corporation, 1993, https://www.rand.org/pubs/notes/N3411.html.

17 See Young C. Kim, 'The Politics of Arms Control in Korea', *Korean Journal of Defense Analysis*, vol. 1, no. 1, 1989, pp. 113–26.

18 James C. Wendt, 'US Conventional Arms Control for Korea: A Proposed Approach', RAND Corporation, 1993, https://www.rand.org/pubs/notes/N3564.html.

19 See Tae-Woong Kim, 'Hanbando pyeonghwacheje ihaeng-ui je munjewa geu haebeob: sinloeguchug cheje jeong-chaggwa nambughan gunbitongjeleul jungsim-eulo' [Unsettled questions of transitioning to a peace system on the Korean Peninsula and the key to its elaboration: centring around the establishment of confidence-building systems and arms control between the two Koreas], *Journal of Peace Studies*, vol. 14, no. 5, 2013, pp. 51–72; Keunyoung Park, 'Korea's Strategy for Institutional Multilateral Security Cooperation in Northeast Asia as a Means to Construct a Peace Regime', *Korea and International Politics*, vol. 22, no. 1, 2006, pp. 199–224; Jaechul Kim et al., 'Nambughan-ui pyeong-hwagongjon-eul wihan un-yongjeog gunbitongje chujinjeonlyag: yuleob CSCEwa jungdong sinaihyeobjeong salyeleul jungsim-eulo' [Promotion strategy for operational arms control for the peaceful coexistence of South and North Korea: focusing on the CSCE and Sinai Agreement], *Journal of Northeast Asian Studies*, vol. 82, 2017, pp. 153–72.; Byungseok Park, 'Dajagan jiyeog-anbohyeoblyeoghoeuiui saengsong-gwa gujo-yuleob-ui gyeongheom-eul tonghan dong-bug-a-eseoui guseongjeonmang' [Multilateral conference for security and cooperation: a study of the European experience and the possibilities for Northeastern Asia], *KRIS Quarterly*, vol. 3, 1994, pp. 291–372; and Seungkeun Lee, 'Construction of the Northeast Asian Multilateral Security System and Conditions of Prior Settlement', *Korean Journal of Area Studies*, vol. 28, no. 1, 2010, pp. 127–51.

20 See Intaek Hyun and Kang Choi, *Arms Control Policies of a New South Korean Government* (Seoul: Korea Research Institute for National Strategy, 2003).

21 See Kim Tae Hyun, 'Nambughan jaelaesig gunbitongje: pyeong-gawa baljeonbanghyang' [Conventional arms control between South Korea and North Korea: assessment and perspective], *Korean Journal of Military Affairs*, vol. 4, 2018, pp. 1–34; Lee Pyo Kyu, 'Gwageowa hyeon munjaein jeongbuui daebug gunbitongje jeobgeunbangbeob bigyo yeongu' [A comparative study on past arms-control approaches toward North Korea through to the Moon government], *Journal of Information and Security*, vol. 19, no. 2, 2019, pp. 147–56; Kang-nyeong Kim, 'Choegeun nambughan gunbitongje-ui chujinhyeonhwang-gwa gwaje' [Recent progress and tasks of arms control in South and North Korea], *Korea and Global Affairs*, vol. 3, no. 2,

2019, pp. 87–130; Jaechul Kim, '9.19 nambuggunsahab-ui ihaengpyeong-gawa hyanghu hanbando gunbitongje chujinbanghyang' [An evaluation of the implementation of the 9.19 South–North Korean military agreement and arms-control strategy on the Korean Peninsula], *Korean Journal of Military Affairs*, vol. 7, 2020, pp. 1–34; Jina Kim, 'Calculating Pyongyang's Next Steps and Coordinating a Response: A South Korean View', in Patrick Cronin (ed.), *Pathways to Peace: Achieving the State Transformation of the Korean Peninsula* (Washington DC: Hudson Institute, 2020), pp. 25–33; and Toby Dalton, 'From Deterrence to Cooperative Security on the Korean Peninsula', *Journal for Peace and Nuclear Disarmament*, vol. 3, no. 1, 2020, pp. 144–56.

22 'Pyongyang Joint Declaration of September 2018', 19 September 2018, available at https://www.ncnk.org/node/1633.

23 Lee Je-hun, 'Seoul's Defense Minister Slams Pyongyang's "Overt Violations" of Inter-Korean Military Agreement', *Hankyoreh*, 17 October 2022, https://english.hani.co.kr/arti/english_edition/e_northkorea/1063016.html.

24 See Lee and Ham, 'South Korea's Conventional Forces Buildup'.

25 See 'At the 8th Congress of the Worker's Party of Korea, a Decision on Revising the Rules of the Worker's Party of Korea Was Adopted', Korean Central News Agency, 10 January 2021.

26 'Nuclear Weapons Policy of the Democratic People's Republic of Korea', *Rodong Sinmun*, 8 September 2022.

27 See Simon Denyer, 'North Korea Wants Security Guarantees, but Can the United States Deliver?', *Washington Post*, 25 April 2019; and Kim Jong-un, speech on the Anniversary of Victory Day, Pyongyang, 27 July 2022.

28 See Emily O. Goldman, 'Arms Control in the Information Age', in Nancy Gallgher (ed.), *Arms Control: New Approaches to Theory and Policy* (Abingdon: Routledge, 1998), p. 43.

29 See James Fearon, 'Signaling Foreign Policy Interests: Tying Hands Versus Sinking Costs', *Journal of Conflict Resolution*, vol. 41, no. 1, February 1997, pp. 68–90.

30 IISS, *The Military Balance 2022* (Abingdon: Routledge for the IISS, 2022), pp. 521–6.

31 Ministry of National Defense, Republic of Korea, 'Defense White Paper 2020', pp. 25–6.

32 *Ibid.*, p. 29.

33 See Lee Young-bin, 'The 2022–2026 Mid-term Defense Plan for Successful Accomplishment of Defense Reform 2.0 and Building a Digitalized Strong Military', *ROK Angle*, no. 240, 24 September 2021.

34 See Kyusup Chung, 'Nambuggibonhab-uiseo: uiuiwa pyeong-ga' [The basic agreements of North and South Korea revisited], *Unification Policy Studies*, vol. 20, no. 1, 2011, pp. 1–24.

35 See Jong Kun Choi, 'Dongbug-a daja-jeog hyeoblyeog jilseo byeonhwawa 6ja hoedam' [Change of Northeast Asia multilateral cooperation and Six-Party Talks], *International Area Studies Review*, vol. 21, no. 1, 2012, pp. 1–24.

36 David Brunnstrom, 'Analysis: Sanctions Fail to Halt North Korea's Accelerating Weapons Programs', Reuters, 7 November

2022, https://www.reuters.com/world/asia-pacific/sanctions-fail-halt-north-koreas-accelerating-weapons-programs-2022-11-04/.

37 See Toby Dalton, Karl Friedhoff and Lami Kim, 'Thinking Nuclear: South Korean Attitudes on Nuclear Weapons', Chicago Council on Global Affairs, February 2022, https://www.thechicagocouncil.org/sites/default/files/2022-02/Korea%20Nuclear%20Report%20PDF.pdf.

Can the New Left Deliver Change in Latin America?

Irene Mia

Latin America has been through a couple of particularly tumultuous years even by its formidable standards. The COVID-19 pandemic aggravated the baleful effects of widespread inequality, large informal markets (which are inefficient), and pre-existing problems associated with the predominant neoliberal economic and development policies. These effects deepened public frustration with traditional politics. A series of elections gave restive voters – voicing the sentiment 'let them all go' (*que se vayan todos*) – the opportunity to effect sweeping political change. In all but one (Nicaragua's) of the nine presidential elections that took place from late 2020 to 2022, incumbents lost their seats, several to fledgling left-wing politicians with iconoclastic, populist agendas that included fairer income distribution.

Demonstrating an intense desire for change, Colombian voters elected the country's first leftist president, Gustavo Petro, and in Brazil former president Luiz Inácio Lula da Silva of the leftist Workers' Party defeated the incumbent, Jair Bolsonaro, after serving 580 days in jail on apparently trumped-up corruption charges. That said, the new 'pink tide' is less cohesive and more fiscally constrained than the one that swept the region in the late 1990s and early 2000s, and it is unclear whether the new governments will be able to make good on their respective mandates.

Irene Mia is an IISS Senior Fellow and Editor of *Armed Conflict Survey*.

Survival | vol. 65 no. 1 | February–March 2023 | pp. 49–56   https://doi.org/10.1080/00396338.2023.2172849

Figure 1: **Support for democracy vs executive coups in the Americas**

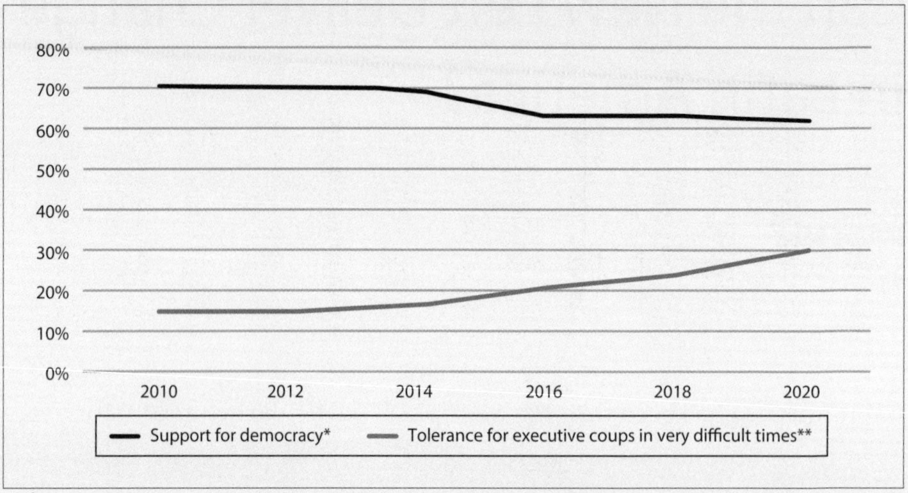

* The data refers to the weighted average per year of responses to the survey question, 'Democracy may have problems, but it is better than any other form of government. To what extent do you agree or disagree with this statement?', with the original scale from 1 to 7 (1 = strongly disagree; 7 = strongly agree) having been rescaled from 0 to 100.
** The data refers to the weighted average per year of the response, 'Yes, it is justified', to the survey question, 'Do you believe that when the country is facing very difficult times, it is justifiable for the executive of the country to close the legislature and govern without the legislature?'
Source: AmericasBarometer, 2010–21, https://public.tableau.com/app/profile/lapop.central/viz/LAPOPV3_2/Combination?publish=yes

Strong impulses, second thoughts

More disturbingly, the fierce desire for rapid change seems to be taking priority over the integrity of the forms and institutions of democracy, with an increasing tolerance for authoritarian practices to address hardships and willingness to accept trade-offs between political rights and socio-economic benefits (see Figure 1). Autocratic populist leaders such as Nayib Bukele in El Salvador and, to a lesser extent, Andrés Manuel López Obrador in Mexico are cases in point. They explicitly embrace political change and enjoy consistently high approval ratings.[1] The midterm elections confirmed their respective parties' dominance. Both, however, are clearly willing to cut democratic corners.

At the same time, societies are polarised across the region (see Figure 2), which is reflected in the political process and in the composition of legislative assemblies. Over the past couple of years, this trend has been apparent in presidential elections, which have often involved run-offs featuring candidates

Figure 2: **Perceived degree of political polarisation in Latin America**

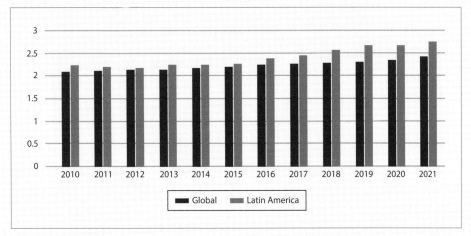

Survey respondents were asked: 'Is society polarised into antagonistic, political camps?' They were offered a choice of five responses, each with a numerical value as follows: 0) Not at all. Supporters of opposing political camps generally interact in a friendly manner. 1) Mainly not. Supporters of opposing political camps are more likely to interact in a friendly than a hostile manner. 2) Somewhat. Supporters of opposing political camps are equally likely to interact in a friendly or hostile manner. 3) Yes, to a noticeable extent. Supporters of opposing political camps are more likely to interact in a hostile than a friendly manner. 4) Yes, to a large extent. Supporters of opposing political camps generally interact in a hostile manner. The data refers to the average response per year.
Source: The V-Dem Dataset, https://v-dem.net/vdemds.html

with diametrically opposed world views and political philosophies. Brazil, Chile and Peru are examples. Such circumstances make consensus-building and institutional effectiveness significantly harder to accomplish.

The recent outcome of the constitutional process in Chile epitomises the enormous challenge of framing and implementing change. Long seen as one of the most economically and politically stable countries in the region, Chile erupted in social protest in late 2019 over inequalities and inadequate basic services. The decision to call a referendum in 2020 for a new constitution, rewritten by a constitutional assembly appointed by Chilean citizens, was widely seen as an intelligent, pragmatic means of channelling protest for greater political participation, enhanced social rights and a more inclusive society into a constructive process. The proposed text was a major departure from the current Pinochet-era constitution, which is based on a minimal-state doctrine and a strong centralised executive. The new draft provided for greater decentralisation, the replacement of the Senate with a 'Chamber of Regions', a larger social state providing basic services (including healthcare and education), and stronger environmental protection. Indigenous rights were a core concern, as the document defined the state as 'plurinational' and called for the judiciary to consider customary law for Indigenous people in rendering judicial decisions. Chile's process had a contagious effect. Demands for new constitutions arose across the region, first in Peru.

In the referendum, however, Chile's draft constitution was rejected by 62% of voters – an especially disconcerting reality given that 80% had also favoured the constitutional process.[2] Several factors help explain this vexing outcome. Firstly, opponents mounted a well-organised 'reject' campaign. Secondly, the language of the proposed constitution was vague, fuelling alarmist interpretations of controversial provisions regarding 'plurination-alism' and social rights, as well as the legislative and justice system. Thirdly, some of the mavericks indulged in unruly and provocative behaviour in the constitutional assembly.[3] Fourthly, the economy's poor performance might have induced voters to use their votes to express frustration with the government, which supported the draft constitution. Finally, high voter turnout inevitably meant a larger moderate contingent.

It is fair to infer that an increasing number of Latin Americans expect a development model whereby income distribution is more equitable and access to basic services and opportunities is more extensive. But Chile's constitutional referendum, in which voting was compulsory, highlighted limits on how radical any new model could be while retaining popular support. Furthermore, it remains unclear how increasingly cash-strapped governments can fund and implement the needed adjustments.

The new leftist wave

Left-of-centre administrations have taken office in the main five economies in the region: Argentina, Brazil, Chile, Colombia and Mexico. Bolivia, Peru and Honduras also followed the trend, even though the latter two had thin leftist traditions. Long-standing leftist governments in Cuba, Nicaragua and Venezuela complete the picture.

The region had not experienced a similar realignment to the left since the 'pink tide' of the late 1990s and early 2000s, when Argentina, Bolivia, Brazil, Chile, Cuba, Ecuador, Paraguay, Peru and Uruguay all had leftist administrations. But there are important differences. The current wave appears less homogeneous than the earlier one, and more strongly rooted in negative anti-incumbent sentiments than affirmatively leftist ones.[4] It stretches from the authoritarian left of Venezuela and Nicaragua to the progressive left of Lula in Brazil, Gabriel Boric in Chile and Petro in Colombia, passing through the 'nostalgic left' of López Obrador and the indigenous-centred left in Bolivia and Peru. It includes all variations, from socially progressive to conservative. Its policy foci range from climate change and social rights to fossil fuels and state-owned enterprises. Often it does not display features traditionally associated with the leftist way of governing. With some exceptions (notably Venezuela and to an extent Argentina), the new pink grouping remains relatively conservative in terms of macroeconomic management and fiscal responsibility, as well as market openness.

Perhaps the greatest difference between the two tides is economic context. The first arose in unique socio-economic circumstances, coinciding with a commodities super-cycle in 2003–10 that afforded governments in the region abundant fiscal resources to address inequalities. Their efforts were successful in the short to medium term, as Latin America was the only region in the world to experience significant declines in inequality and poverty in 2000–15.[5] But once the commodity boom ended, excessively generous spending and limited savings made prevailing policies unsustainable and ushered in conservative governments in most Latin American countries.

By contrast, at present the region is experiencing the double shock of the pandemic and the energy crunch occasioned by the Russia–Ukraine war, with over 40% of the population facing moderate or severe food insecurity, the highest level since 2014, against a backdrop of high inflation, shrinking fiscal space and sluggish global demand. This makes addressing inequalities far more difficult, all the more so in politically divided countries. Their voters are less patient, and approval ratings for several newly elected officials have steeply plunged.[6] Yet long time frames are needed to strengthen the foundations for sustainable growth, which is a precondition for a more inclusive development model. Successful governments would have to address perennial shortcomings in education and innovation systems, infrastructure and the functioning of markets, while ameliorating macroeconomic imbalances in the shorter term.

Glimmers of hope?

Although quick change will be close to impossible for most governments in the region, there are some bright spots. Shared views among the new governments about foreign policy could produce greater regional alignment in external relations and increase the region's global leverage. For instance, the focus on climate by Lula, Petro and Boric could catalyse a common position on climate-related loss and damage visited on the Global South by the Global North, and related liabilities. This could result in more international climate funding for adaptation. Petro's recent calls for a 'debt-for-nature' swap to protect the Amazon rainforest represents an interesting and relevant overture.[7] Under such an arrangement, countries in the Amazon region could restructure their debt on more favourable terms (lower interest rates or longer maturity) and use the corresponding proceeds for adaptation or conservation projects. Lula's proposal for a so-called 'OPEC for rainforests' could help boost conservation efforts worldwide by coordinating approaches among Brazil, the Democratic Republic of the Congo and Indonesia, which account for most of the world's rainforests.

The region's large endowment of critical minerals for the clean-energy transition is another promising area of cooperation. With Argentina, Bolivia, Chile, Mexico and Peru collectively representing two-thirds of global lithium reserves, a coordinated stance by their governments on lithium exploitation and commercialisation could enable these countries to reap maximum benefits from a natural asset for domestic development. The lithium cartel proposed by López Obrador would be counterproductive in the long run; challenges of exploitation remain huge; and the regional track record in preserving commodity windfalls for rainy days is not strong.[8] But a concerted approach could produce better negotiated conditions, facilitate the sharing of expertise and perhaps optimise lithium value chains in the region, increasing intra-regional trade, which is key for economic and trade diversification, and durable growth.[9]

Finally, potential alignment on new approaches and solutions to spiralling drug-related violence and conflict in the region – a major driver of regional and global instability and a key concern for voters – could usefully unite the new governments. Petro's calls for rethinking the US-supported hardline 'war on drugs' approach in favour of a more comprehensive one that also addresses root causes (including land redistribution) is gaining traction in the region.[10] Such an approach, if implemented correctly, could reduce violence while alleviating socio-economic inequalities.

Notes

1   See, for example, Eddie Galdamez, 'Nayib Bukele Approval Rating. 8.42 Score out of 10 in the Latest Survey!', El Salvador INFO, 10 November 2022, https://elsalvadorinfo.net/nayib-bukele-approval-rate/; and Carin Zissis, 'Approval Tracker: Mexico's President AMLO', Americas Society/Council of the Americas, 6 December 2022, https://www.as-coa.org/articles/approval-tracker-mexicos-president-amlo.

2   See 'Chile Overwhelmingly Rejects Progressive New Constitution', Reuters, 5 September 2022, https://www.reuters.com/world/americas/chileans-head-polls-decide-progressive-new-constitution-2022-09-04/.

3   See 'REACTION: Chile Rejects New Constitution', Americas Quarterly, 5 September 2022, https://www.americasquarterly.org/article/reaction-chile-rejects-new-constitution/.

4   See, for instance, Santiago Leiras, 'New Left Turn in Latin America, Which Left?', Latinoamérica21, 20 July 2022, https://latinoamerica21.com/en/new-left-turn-in-latin-america-which-left/.

5   See, for example, Ravi Balakrishnan et al., 'Commodity Cycles, Inequality, and Poverty in Latin America', International Monetary Fund, Western Hemisphere Department, No. 21/09, 2021.

6   See 'Latam Presidential Ranking: Jul/Aug 2022', Directorio Legislativo, https://directoriolegislativo.org/en/latam-presidential-ranking-jul-aug-2022/.

7   See Sebastian Rodriguez, 'Colombia's New President Calls for Debt Swap to Protect the Amazon', Climate Home News, 8 October 2022, https://www.climatechangenews.com/2022/08/10/colombias-new-president-debt-swap-protect-amazon-rainforest/.

8   See Michael Stott, 'State Looms over Latin America's Hopes to Exploit "White Gold" of Lithium', Mexico News Daily, 14 February 2022, https://mexiconewsdaily.com/opinion/state-looms-over-latin-americas-hopes-to-exploit-white-gold-of-lithium/.

9   See Irene Mia, 'Latin America Will Need a Smart Approach to Trade in the Post Covid-19 World', London School of Economics Blog, 13 December 2021, https://blogs.lse.ac.uk/latamcaribbean/2021/12/13/latin-america-will-need-a-smart-approach-to-trade-in-the-post-covid-19-world/.

10 See, for example, 'Colombia Breaks Coca-growing Record, US-led War on Drugs "Failure", Says Govt', MSN, 21 October 2022, https://www.msn.com/en-gb/news/world/colombia-breaks-coca-growing-record-us-led-war-on-drugs-failure-says-govt/ar-AA13clSM.

The Crowded Red Sea

Camille Lons and Benjamin Petrini

The Red Sea region has come into sharper strategic focus for great powers as well as regional powers.[1] This is not surprising. Some 12% of global seaborne trade and 40% of Europe's trade with Asia and the Middle East, as well as 8% of seaborne hydrocarbons, pass through the Red Sea. In March 2021, the accidental six-day blocking of the Suez Canal by the cargo ship *Ever Given* demonstrated how traumatic such a closure could be for global supply chains. Furthermore, the 15 cables that cross Egypt between the Mediterranean and the Red seas, and those that run under the Red Sea and the Gulf of Aden, handle an estimated one-third of the world's internet traffic.[2]

Yet it is a chronically underdeveloped, conflict-ridden and unstable region. Ethiopia, Somalia and Yemen are among the top ten states on the International Rescue Committee's watchlist for humanitarian emergency.[3] Djibouti, Egypt, Eritrea, Ethiopia, Jordan, Somalia, Sudan and Yemen are facing economic and food-security crises, with some areas on the verge of famine. Several Red Sea countries are among the worst in terms of economic and human-development standards.[4] Ethiopia remains engaged in a decade-long diplomatic conflict over the Grand Ethiopian Renaissance Dam (GERD) with Egypt and Sudan, which perceive the project as a dire threat to their water security.

In 2021, one in four of the world's conflict fatalities occurred in Red Sea countries.[5] The Red Sea is a major hub of global arms trafficking and smuggling by both state and non-state actors, which feeds existing conflicts and

Camille Lons is an IISS Research Associate. **Benjamin Petrini** is IISS Research Fellow for Conflict, Security and Development.

Survival | vol. 65 no. 1 | February–March 2023 | pp. 57–67   https://doi.org/10.1080/00396338.2023.2172851

exacerbates state fragility. For example, Iran has made the southern Red Sea and the Gulf of Aden key routes for smuggling weapons to Yemen.[6] Some of them have ended up in the hands of al-Shabaab militants in Somalia.[7] Ethiopia's internal turmoil and civil war in Tigray, which tentatively ended with a peace agreement in November 2022, add uncertainty to the regional security outlook. Other threats, including Somalia-based piracy and jihadist militancy, also plague the region.

Against this forbidding backdrop, overlapping rivalries involving Iran, Israel and the Gulf Cooperation Council (GCC) countries pose risks of intensifying regional discord.

Iranian persistence, Saudi and Emirati ascendancy

In decades past, Iran cultivated political ties with Red Sea countries such as Sudan and Eritrea, taking advantage of their shared diplomatic ostracism, in its quest for strategic depth and corridors for delivering assistance and resources to its allies and proxies.[8] Tehran also built up its naval capability in the region – including in the Bab el-Mandeb Strait, which connects the Gulf of Aden with the Red Sea – to protect Iranian oil tankers and commercial vessels, and to increase its strategic leverage by holding oil shipments at risk.[9] A resurgent Iranian threat in the southern Red Sea has encouraged Saudi Arabia and Israel to enhance naval security cooperation. In July 2022, Benny Gantz, then Israeli defence minister, stated that Israel had 'identified the most significant Iranian military presence in the area in the past decade'.[10]

Yemen remains a soft entry point for Iranian influence in the region. In Yemen's civil war, a Saudi- and United Arab Emirates (UAE)-led coalition backed by France, the United Kingdom and the United States, and including nine countries from the region, has supported the putative regime against the Iran-backed Houthis, who have controlled Sana'a since 2015. After years of military stalemate and humanitarian crisis, Saudi Arabia de-escalated in 2020, but the Houthis attacked the oil-rich province of Marib in 2021 and stepped up attacks on the fragmented unity government based in Aden, as well as Saudi Arabia and the UAE.[11] Houthi officials have threatened to target Israel on several occasions.[12] More broadly, instability in Yemen is threatening freedom of navigation in the southern Red Sea. Between January 2018 and October 2022, the Houthis executed at least 26 attacks against commercial vessels and civilian port infrastructure in the Red Sea.[13]

Heightened Saudi and Emirati involvement in the Red Sea region emerged before their intervention in Yemen against the Houthis and, by extension, Iran. Egypt had traditionally been the strongest Arab country in the Red Sea region, hosting the Arab League and leading wars against Israel in 1956, 1967 and 1973. The second of these had a Red Sea *casus belli* – Egypt's closing of the Strait of Tiran to Israeli shipping – and the war that ensued transformed the Middle East. The 1978 Camp David Accords, which led, a year later, to formal peace between Egypt and Israel, also secured permanent US military support and anchored the US security architecture in the region. The fall of Egyptian president Hosni Mubarak in 2011 during the Arab Spring uprisings, however, afforded Saudi Arabia an opportunity to assume an increasingly prominent role in the Red Sea region. Both Saudi Arabia and the UAE directly supported the coup that overthrew the Muslim Brotherhood's chaotic post-Mubarak government and installed General Abdel Fattah Al-Sisi, who was dependent on Saudi support and preoccupied with reconstructing Egypt's domestic order.

Saudi ambitions in what was once Egypt's *chasse gardée* are changing the security balance in the Red Sea. The Kingdom has launched a series of mega-projects on its Red Sea coast, including the $500 billion NEOM smart city. In 2020, it also inaugurated a new Red Sea Council, rebranding what was originally an Egyptian initiative. If completed, Egypt's planned handover to Saudi Arabia of the islands of Tiran and Sanafir – which are strategically located at the entrance of the Gulf of Aqaba and flank Israel's Red Sea port of Eilat – would further strengthen Riyadh's strategic position on the Red Sea.

Over the past decade, Saudi Arabia and the UAE have played an increasingly prominent role in Horn of Africa politics. Helped by South Sudan's 2011 secession and Sudan's subsequent loss of oil revenues, the two Gulf Arab countries have driven a wedge between Khartoum and Tehran.[14] Since former Sudanese president Omar al-Bashir's political demise in 2019, Riyadh and Abu Dhabi have significantly shaped Sudanese politics, discreetly supporting the generals who engineered the

October 2021 military coup. The coup embarrassed them, however, and they subsequently joined the US and the UK in calls for the restoration of civilian rule and extended mediation efforts, which culminated in an agreement, in December 2022, for a civilian government and free elections. Similarly, Riyadh and Abu Dhabi were the main sponsors of the historic 2018 peace agreement between Ethiopia and Eritrea, and their recent courtship of Eritrea with infrastructure investment and financial aid displaced its cooperation with Iran in trade, energy and infrastructure, as well as security and military affairs. Similar dynamics have taken hold with respect to Djibouti and Somalia.

Saudi Arabia and the UAE have also challenged and blunted the regional influence of Qatar and Turkey, which had partnered in an attempt to establish a revisionist bloc in the region, and tamped down Qatar's designs on supposedly Iran-friendly (but apparently merely Muslim Brotherhood-friendly) strategic independence there, particularly in the Horn of Africa.

Strategic location and militarisation

Because the Red Sea is a strategic line of communication connecting the Mediterranean Sea with the Indian Ocean, great powers have traditionally established a presence in the region – often a military one. There are ten foreign countries with a military presence in the Red Sea and the Gulf of Aden.[15] The UAE opened a base in Assab, Eritrea, in 2015, using it mainly for air and naval operations against the Houthis. Turkey has a base in Somalia. For external actors such as China, Turkey and the UAE, a ramped-up military presence has coincided with the expansion of foreign direct investment in ports and transport infrastructure, real estate and construction.[16] Through DP World, for example, the Emiratis have secured port access in Eritrea and Somalia, as well as Sudan.

Djibouti is especially prized, its location enabling it to exact considerable strategic rent from outside actors. With a landmass the size of Vermont and a GDP equal to Andorra's, it is situated on the Bab el-Mandeb Strait, the key international choke point on the southern end of the Red Sea. Because its narrowest opening is only 29 kilometres wide, the strait is vulnerable to blockade and military escalation. In 2018, a series of Houthi attacks against tankers passing through the strait led Saudi Arabia to temporarily halt its oil shipments through the Red Sea.[17]

Djibouti has hosted Combined Joint Task Force – Horn of Africa, the United States' largest military base in Africa, since 2002, and has served as a key hub for multinational counter-piracy operations for 15 years. Since 2017, it has been the site of China's only overseas military base, which is being upgraded to accommodate an aircraft carrier.[18] France has had a base there since 1946 (when Djibouti was still a French colony), Japan since 2011 and Italy since 2013. Troops from Germany and Spain are also present. Russia sees the Red Sea as a key point of access to the Indian Ocean for its Black Sea Fleet and has sought to establish a base in Djibouti, but the US blocked its bid to do so in 2014.[19] In 2020, Khartoum approved a project for a Russian base in Port Sudan, but its implementation stalled after the military coup of October 2021.[20]

China is a key economic actor in the Red Sea, as an estimated 60% of Chinese goods shipped to Europe pass through the Suez Canal.[21] Through Chinese investments in roads, railways, energy and communications, Ethiopia and Djibouti have become China's biggest beneficiaries in the Horn. Other regional governments appear eager to develop ties with Beijing in response to perceived American retrenchment, and China has increased its influence in the region. China owns nearly 60% of Djibouti's foreign debt.[22] The opening of its military base there has amplified unease about inordinate Chinese leverage. Beijing has ramped up port calls and naval exercises with Red Sea states, and taken part in the development, financing and operation of numerous port infrastructure and storage facilities on Red Sea coasts, including significant investments around the Suez Canal.[23] Red Sea countries have thus far resisted attempts to politicise maritime access. Egypt, for example, has firmly rejected calls to restrict the passage of Russian ships through the Suez Canal.[24] But resistance could buckle if Egypt perceives its core interests to be at stake.

US involvement

During and immediately after the Cold War, the US dominated the Red Sea region. After 9/11, blowback from the US-led 'war on terror' – especially the Iraq War and the reactivation of the Israeli–Palestinian conflict – eroded the United States' influence in the region. Iranian activity in the region and Israeli and Gulf Arab responses, however, have revived US strategic interest. The US has prioritised empowering its regional partners and strengthening emerging Israel–Gulf security synergies to counteract Iran's activities. The establishment of a Chinese base in Djibouti in 2017 and the growing economic influence of Chinese companies in the region have also prompted Washington to reaffirm its presence and support. In the medium term, however, the Russia–Ukraine war, European security exigencies and Indo-Pacific challenges could limit US attention to the region, and deteriorating US–Saudi relations could inhibit US traction there.[25]

Nevertheless, the Biden administration is looking to establish greater American control in the region, albeit largely from over the horizon. In May 2022, the White House reversed the Trump administration's decision to pull out of Somalia and approved the redeployment of US troops there to continue countering al-Shabaab.[26] In July, Washington sent Mike Hammer, the newly appointed special envoy for the Horn of Africa, to relaunch negotiations on the GERD and support the peaceful resolution of Ethiopia's war in Tigray, as to which combatants reached a peace agreement in November 2022.

The Biden administration has also been promoting greater security cooperation between Israel and other Red Sea powers by leveraging the 2020 Abraham Accords. Beginning in 2021, Israel sharply increased its naval operations in the Red Sea region in response to Iran's activities in the southern part of the waterway.[27] In March 2022, the US convened a secret meeting of top military officials from Bahrain, Egypt, Israel, Jordan, Qatar, Saudi Arabia and the UAE in the Egyptian Red Sea resort of Sharm al-Sheikh to explore modes of coordination against Iran's growing missile and drone capabilities.[28] A month before, Israel and the UAE explored the possibility of deploying Israeli radars to the UAE after it experienced a series of Houthi attacks.[29]

In addition, Washington is encouraging naval cooperation and including Israel in regional initiatives. In November 2021, the US led the first quadrilateral naval drill in the Red Sea with the participation of Bahrain, Israel and the UAE in response to Iranian attacks on Israeli naval assets.[30] Less than three months later, Israel took part in another major US-led naval exercise in the Red Sea that included Saudi Arabia and Oman.[31] Washington has since announced the creation of a new international Red Sea task force including Israel as well as Egypt to counter illicit smuggling, and another to deploy and test uninhabited seaborne drones. Redrawing US Central Command's area of responsibility to include Israel in September 2021 has reinforced the disposition favouring inclusive multilateral naval cooperation.[32]

*   *   *

In reaffirming a commitment to Red Sea security and signalling its determination to address Iranian threats of regional disruption, Washington's apparent intention is to foster the emergence of a new security architecture, anchored by US-empowered regional partners while reflecting greater regional security autonomy based in part on closer security ties between Israel and the Gulf Arab countries. Yet Biden heavily criticised the Saudi intervention in Yemen and started his presidency with the partial suspension of US military aid to the Kingdom. While the White House has softened its criticism for pragmatic reasons, its discomfort with Saudi and Emirati policies in Somalia and Sudan, as well as Yemen, is likely to continue.[33]

More broadly, whereas the US prioritises the containment of Iran in the region, Israel is focused sharply on stopping the Iranian nuclear programme, and the Gulf Arab states on curtailing Iran's regional influence through proxies, non-state armed groups, and missile and drone capabilities. Given the potential divergence between American and regional concerns, neither US nor regional involvement appears likely to lend stability to the Red Sea region.

Notes

1. As contemplated here, the region includes 12 countries: Djibouti, Egypt, Eritrea, Ethiopia, Israel, Jordan, Qatar, Saudi Arabia, Somalia, Sudan, the United Arab Emirates and Yemen.
2. See, for example, United States Institute of Peace, 'Final Report and Recommendations of the Senior Study Group on Peace and Security in the Red Sea Arena', 29 October 2020, https://www.usip.org/publications/2020/10/final-report-and-recommendations-senior-study-group-peace-and-security-red-sea.

3   International Rescue Committee, 'Emergency Watchlist 2023', http://www.rescue.org/sites/default/files/2022-12/CS2301_Watchlist%20Project_Report_Final_0.pdf.

4   See UN Development Programme, 'Human Development Insights', http://hdr.undp.org/en/content/latest-human-development-index-ranking.

5   See Armed Conflict Location and Event Data Project (ACLED), 'ACLED 2021: The Year in Review', March 2022, https://acleddata.com/acleddatanew/wp-content/uploads/2022/03/ACLED_Annual_Year-in-Review-2021_Web_Pub_Fin-.pdf.

6   See Benoit Faucon and Dion Nissenbaum, 'Iran Navy Port Emerges as Key to Alleged Weapons Smuggling to Yemen, U.N. Report Says', *Wall Street Journal*, 9 January 2022, https://www.wsj.com/articles/iran-navy-port-emerges-as-key-to-alleged-weapons-smuggling-to-yemen-u-n-report-says-11641651941.

7   See Katharine Houreld, 'Iranian-supplied Arms Smuggled from Yemen into Somalia, Study Says', Reuters, 10 November 2021, https://www.reuters.com/world/iranian-supplied-arms-smuggled-yemen-into-somalia-study-says-2021-11-10/.

8   See Soli Shahvar, 'Iran's Global Reach: The Islamic Republic of Iran's Policy, Involvement, and Activity in Africa', *DOMES Digest of Middle East Studies*, vol. 29, no. 1, March 2020, pp. 53–75.

9   See Mahsa Rouhi, 'US–Iran Tensions and the Oil Factor', *Survival*, vol. 60, no. 5, October–November 2018, pp. 33–40.

10 Emanuel Fabian, 'Gantz: Iran's Maritime Activity in Red Sea is "Most Significant" in a Decade', *Times of Israel*, 5 July 2022, https://www.timesofisrael.com/gantz-irans-maritime-activity-in-red-sea-is-most-significant-in-a-decade/.

11 See Seth G. Jones et al., 'The Iranian and Houthi War Against Saudi Arabia', CSIS Brief, Center for Strategic & International Studies, December 2021, https://csis-website-prod.s3.amazonaws.com/s3fs-public/publication/211221_Jones_IranianHouthi_SaudiArabia.pdf?fn1d98tAhj7yOUr.IncppMueLOC4kv83.

12 See, for example, Seth J. Frantzman, 'Houthis Renew Threats to UAE, Saudi Arabia and Israel', *Jerusalem Post*, 7 October 2022, https://www.jpost.com/middle-east/article-719136.

13 Data compiled by the authors from the Global Terrorism Database, https://www.start.umd.edu/gtd/; UN Security Council, 'Final Report of the Panel of Experts on Yemen', S/2022/50, 26 January 2022, https://www.securitycouncilreport.org/atf/cf/%7B65BFCF9B-6D27-4E9C-8CD3-CF6E4FF96FF9%7D/S_2022_50.pdf; and 2022 media reports.

14 See Giorgio Cafiero, 'Is a Sudanese–Iranian Rapprochement Possible?', Middle East Institute, 9 May 2019, https://www.mei.edu/publications/sudanese-iranian-rapprochement-possible.

15 See Zach Vertin, 'Red Sea Rivalries: The Gulf States Are Playing a Dangerous Game in the Horn of Africa', *Foreign Affairs*, 15 January 2019, https://www.foreignaffairs.com/articles/east-africa/2019-01-15/red-sea-rivalries.

16 Between 2000 and 2017, Gulf countries invested $13bn in the Horn of

Africa and disbursed $6.6bn in official development assistance. See John Calabrese, 'The Bab el-Mandeb Strait: Regional and Great Power Rivalries on the Shores of the Red Sea', Middle East Institute, 29 January 2020, https://www.mei.edu/publications/bab-el-mandeb-strait-regional-and-great-power-rivalries-shores-red-sea.

[17] See David Sheppard, 'Saudi Arabia Suspends Red Sea Oil Shipments Following Attack', *Financial Times*, 25 July 2018, https://www.ft.com/content/45c18e00-904f-11e8-b639-7680cedcc421.

[18] See Brian Gicheru Kinyua, 'New Pier at China's Djibouti Base Could Accommodate Carriers', *Maritime Executive*, 30 April 2021, https://maritime-executive.com/article/new-pier-at-china-s-djibouti-base-could-accommodate-carriers.

[19] See Zach Vertin, 'Great Power Rivalry in the Red Sea: China's Experiment in Djibouti and Implications for the United States', Global China, June 2020, https://www.brookings.edu/wp-content/uploads/2020/06/FP_20200615_china_djibouti_vertin.pdf.

[20] See Amy Mackinnon, Robbie Gramer and Jack Detsch, 'Russia's Dreams of a Red Sea Naval Base Are Scuttled – for Now', *Foreign Policy*, 15 July 2022, https://foreignpolicy.com/2022/07/15/russia-sudan-putin-east-africa-port-red-sea-naval-base-scuttled/. Moscow held initial discussions with Eritrea for a military base, but to no apparent avail.

[21] See John C.K. Daly, 'Suez Closure Brightens the Future of China's New Silk Road', *China Brief*, Jamestown Foundation, vol. 21, no. 11, 7 June 2021, https://jamestown.org/program/suez-closure-brightens-the-future-of-chinas-new-silk-road/.

[22] See, for instance, IISS, *China's Belt and Road Initiative: A Geopolitical and Geo-economic Assessment* (London: IISS, November 2022), https://www.iiss.org/publications/strategic-dossiers/chinas-belt-and-road-initiative.

[23] See Joel Wuthnow, 'The PLA Beyond Asia: China's Growing Military Presence in the Red Sea Region', INSS Strategic Forum, National Defense University, January 2020, p. 7, https://www.ndu.edu/Portals/68/Documents/stratforum/SF-303.pdf.

[24] Mohammad Hanafi, 'Suez Canal Authority Remains Neutral in Russian–Ukrainian War', *Al-Monitor*, 9 March 2022, https://www.al-monitor.com/originals/2022/03/suez-canal-authority-remains-neutral-russian-ukrainian-war.

[25] See, for instance, Emile Hokayem, 'Fraught Relations: Saudi Ambitions and American Anger', *Survival*, vol. 64, no. 6, December 2022–January 2023, pp. 7–22.

[26] Charlie Savage and Eric Schmitt, 'Biden Approves Plan to Redeploy Several Hundred Ground Forces into Somalia', *New York Times*, 16 May 2022, https://www.nytimes.com/2022/05/16/us/politics/biden-military-somalia.html.

[27] See Josef Federman, 'With Eye on Iran, Israeli Navy Steps Up Red Sea Presence', Associated Press, 16 September 2021, https://apnews.com/article/middle-east-business-iran-israel-navy-4ece4ff6a5b881e8cd3d8884110f6271.

[28] See Michael R. Gordon and David S. Cloud, 'U.S. Held Secret Meeting with Israeli, Arab Military Chiefs to

Counter Iran Air Threat', *Wall Street Journal*, 26 June 2022, https://www.wsj.com/articles/u-s-held-secret-meeting-with-israeli-arab-military-chiefs-to-counter-iran-air-threat-11656235802.

29 See Arie Egozi, 'UAE, Reeling from Houthi Attacks, Seeking Israeli Advanced Radar: Sources', *Breaking Defense*, 1 February 2022, https://breakingdefense.com/2022/02/uae-reeling-from-houthi-attacks-seeking-israeli-advanced-radar-sources/.

30 'UAE, Bahrain, Israel and U.S. Forces in First Joint Naval Drill', Reuters, 11 November 2021, https://www.reuters.com/world/middle-east/uae-bahrain-israel-us-forces-conduct-red-sea-military-exercise-2021-11-11/.

31 Lisa Barrington, 'Israel Participates in Huge U.S. Mideast Naval Exercise Alongside Saudi, Oman', Reuters, 2 February 2022, https://www.reuters.com/world/middle-east/israel-participates-huge-us-gulf-naval-exercise-alongside-saudi-oman-2022-02-02/.

32 See Seth J. Frantzman, 'US Central Command Absorbs Israel into Its Area of Responsibility', *Defense News*, 7 September 2021, https://www.defensenews.com/global/mideast-africa/2021/09/07/us-central-command-absorbs-israel-into-its-area-of-responsibility/.

33 See Samer Al-Atrush and Felicia Schwartz, 'Biden's About-turn on Saudi War in Yemen', *Financial Times*, 27 June 2022, https://www.ft.com/content/ae4db53a-a17e-4c9d-ae40-ff0c00d3fcf9.

Noteworthy

Zelenskyy's appeal

'Dear Americans, in all states, cities and communities, all those who value freedom and justice, who cherish it as strongly as we Ukrainians in our cities, in each and every family, I hope my words of respect and gratitude resonate in each American heart.

[…]

Against all odds and doom-and-gloom scenarios, Ukraine didn't fall. Ukraine is alive and kicking. Thank you. And it gives me good reason to share with you our first joint victory: we defeated Russia in the battle for minds of the world. We have no fear, nor should anyone in the world have it. Ukrainians gained this victory, and it gives us courage which inspires the entire world.

Americans gained this victory, and that's why you have succeeded in uniting the global community to protect freedom and international law. Europeans gained this victory, and that's why Europe is now stronger and more independent than ever. The Russian tyranny has lost control over us. And it will never influence our minds again.

Yet, we have to do whatever it takes to ensure that countries of the Global South also gain such victory. I know one more, I think very important, thing: the Russians will stand a chance to be free only when they defeat the Kremlin in their minds. Yet, the battle continues, and we have to defeat the Kremlin on the battlefield, yes.

This battle is not only for the territory, for this or another part of Europe. The battle is not only for life, freedom and security of Ukrainians or any other nation which Russia attempts to conquer. This struggle will define in what world our children and grandchildren will live, and then their children and grandchildren. It will define whether it will be a democracy for Ukrainians and for Americans – for all.

This battle cannot be frozen or postponed. It cannot be ignored, hoping that the ocean or something else will provide a protection. From the United States to China, from Europe to Latin America, and from Africa to Australia, the world is too interconnected and interdependent to allow someone to stay aside and at the same time to feel safe when such a battle continues.

Our two nations are allies in this battle. And next year will be a turning point, I know it, the point when Ukrainian courage and American resolve must guarantee the future of our common freedom, the freedom of people who stand for their values.

Ladies and gentlemen … yesterday before coming here to Washington DC, I was at the front line in our Bakhmut. In our stronghold in the east of Ukraine, in the Donbas. The Russian military and mercenaries have been attacking Bakhmut nonstop since May. They have been attacking it day and night, but Bakhmut stands.

Last year, 70,000 people lived here in Bakhmut, in this city, and now only few civilians stay. Every inch of that land is soaked in blood; roaring guns sound every hour. Trenches in the Donbas change hands several times a day in fierce combat, and even hand fighting. But the Ukrainian Donbas stands.

Russians use everything, everything they have against Bakhmut and our other beautiful cities. The occupiers have a significant advantage in artillery. They have an advantage in ammunition. They have much more missiles and planes than we ever had. It's true, but our defence forces stand. And we all are proud of them.

The Russians' tactic is primitive. They burn down and destroy everything they see. They sent thugs to the front lines. They sent convicts to the war. They threw everything against us, similar to the other tyranny, which in the Battle of the Bulge threw everything it had against the free world. Just like the brave American soldiers which held their lines and fought back [Adolf] Hitler's forces during the Christmas of 1944, brave Ukrainian soldiers are doing the same to [Vladimir] Putin's forces this Christmas.

Ukraine holds its lines and will never surrender. So, here is the front line, the tyranny which has no lack of cruelty against the lives of free people – and your support is crucial, not just to stand in such fights but to get to the turning point to win on the battlefield.

We have artillery, yes. Thank you. We have it. Is it enough? Honestly, not really. To ensure Bakhmut is not just a stronghold that holds back the Russian Army, but for the Russian Army to completely pull out, more cannons and shells are needed. If so, just like the Battle of Saratoga, the fight for Bakhmut will change the trajectory of our war for independence and for freedom.

If your *Patriots* stop the Russian terror against our cities, it will let Ukrainian patriots work to the full to defend our freedom. When Russia cannot reach our cities by its artillery, it tries to destroy them with missile attacks. More than that, Russia found an ally in this genocidal policy: Iran. Iranian deadly drones sent to Russia in hundreds became a threat to our critical infrastructure. That is how one terrorist has found the other.

It is just a matter of time [before] they will strike against your other allies if we do not stop them now. We must do it. I believe there should be no taboos between us in our alliance. Ukraine never asked the American soldiers to fight on our land instead of us. I assure you that Ukrainian soldiers can perfectly operate American tanks and planes themselves.

Financial assistance is also critically important, and I would like to thank you, thank you very much, thank you for both financial packages you have already provided us with and the ones you may be willing to decide on. Your money is not charity. It's an investment in the global security and democracy that we handle in the most responsible way.

Russia could stop its aggression, really, if it wanted to, but you can speed up our victory. I know it. And it will prove to any potential aggressor that no one can succeed in breaking national borders, no one committing atrocities and reigning over people against their will. It would be naive to wait for steps towards peace from Russia, which enjoys being a terrorist state. Russians are still poisoned by the Kremlin.

The restoration of international legal order is our joint task. We need peace, yes. Ukraine has already offered proposals, which I just discussed with President [Joe] Biden, our peace formula, ten points which should and must be implemented for our joint security, guaranteed for decades ahead and the summit which can be held.

I'm glad to say that President Biden supported our peace initiative today. Each of you, ladies and gentlemen, can assist in the implementation to ensure that America's leadership remains solid, bicameral and bipartisan. Thank you.

You can strengthen sanctions to make Russia feel how ruinous its aggression truly is. It is in your power, really, to help us bring to justice everyone who started this unprovoked and criminal war. Let's do it. Let the terrorist state be held responsible for its terror and aggression and compensate all losses done by this war. Let the world see that the United States are here.

Ladies and gentlemen … in two days we will celebrate Christmas. Maybe candlelit. Not because it's more romantic, no, but because there will be no electricity. Millions won't have neither heating nor running water. All of this will be the result of Russian missile and drone attacks on our energy infrastructure.

But we do not complain. We do not judge and compare whose life is easier. Your well-being is the product of your national security; the result of your struggle for independence and your many victories. We, Ukrainians, will also go through our war of independence and freedom with dignity and success.

We'll celebrate Christmas. Celebrate Christmas and, even if there is no electricity, the light of our faith in ourselves will not be put out … Millions of Ukrainians, wish the same: victory. Only victory.

We already built [a] strong Ukraine, with strong people, strong army, strong institutions together with you. We developed strong security guarantees for our country and for entire Europe and the world, together with you. And also together with you, we'll put in place everyone who will defy freedom. This will be the basis to protect democracy in Europe and the world over.

Now, on this special Christmas time, I want to thank you, all of you. I thank every American family which cherishes the warmth of its home and wishes the same warmth to other people. I thank President Biden and both parties, at the Senate and the House, for your invaluable assistance. I thank your cities and your citizens who supported Ukraine this year, who hosted our Ukrainians, our people, who waved our national flags, who acted to help us. Thank you all, from everyone who is now at the front line, from everyone who is awaiting victory.

Standing here today, I recall the words of the president Franklin Delano Roosevelt, which are I think so good for this moment: "The American people, in their righteous might, will win through to absolute victory." The Ukrainian people will win, too, absolutely.

I know that everything depends on us, on Ukrainian armed forces, yet so much depends on the world. So much in the world depends on you. When I was in Bakhmut yesterday, our heroes gave me the flag, the battle flag, the flag of those who defend Ukraine, Europe and the world at the cost of their lives. They asked me to bring this flag to you, to the US Congress, to members of the House of Representatives and senators whose decisions can save millions of people.

So, let these decisions be taken. Let this flag stay with you, ladies and gentlemen. This flag is a symbol of our victory in this war. We stand, we fight and we will win because we are united – Ukraine, America and the entire free world.

Just one thing, if I can, the last thing – thank you so much, may God protect our brave troops and citizens, may God forever bless the United States of America. Merry Christmas and a happy, victorious New Year. *Slava Ukraini*!'

Ukrainian President Volodymyr Zelenskyy addresses a joint session of the US Congress in Washington DC on 20 December 2022.[1]

Sources
1   President of Ukraine, 'We Stand, We Fight and We Will Win', 22 December 2022, https://www.president.gov.ua/en/news/mi-stoyimo-boremos-i-vigrayemo-bo-mi-razom-ukrayina-amerika-80017; and 'Full Transcript of Zelensky's Speech Before Congress', *New York Times*, 21 December 2022, https://www.nytimes.com/2022/12/21/us/politics/zelensky-speech-transcript.html.

Europe's Fragile Unity

Arlo Poletti

There is little doubt that the Russia–Ukraine war represents the hardest of the many tests that Europe has faced over the past few decades, one that could not just lead European governments to temporarily quarrel and vacillate, but also cause the European Union to disintegrate altogether.

Over the course of a year, the war has produced enormous economic strain. The escalating energy crisis has increased upward pressure on inflation, and is likely to throw Europe into a recessionary spiral with the possibility of stagflation. Entire economic sectors in key European industrial countries are facing existential challenges, with small and medium enterprises struggling to survive as production and borrowing costs have spiked and individual and household consumption has plummeted. Disruptions in the flow of electronics, raw materials and spare parts emanating from China and other emerging markets has diminished many European firms' global trade positions and forced them to recalibrate or reconsider their long-standing supply chains and partnerships.

Politically, the crisis is exacerbating some of Europe's long-lasting political cleavages and creating new ones. Differences in fiscal capacity and access to capital markets are reviving the north–south divisions that almost put an end to the eurozone. New geopolitical fissures over how to deal with

Arlo Poletti is an associate professor of political science and international relations at the Department of Sociology and Social Research of the University of Trento.

Survival | vol. 65 no. 1 | February–March 2023 | pp. 71–80   https://doi.org/10.1080/00396338.2023.2172854

the Russian threat are deepening between eastern and western member states, with the former group, including the Baltic states and Poland, calling for unfettered military support to Ukraine and the latter group, including France, Germany and Italy, more open to a negotiated settlement.

Notwithstanding these strains, many commentators remain optimistic about Europe's resilience. Two sets of arguments underpin this optimism. One is based on the observation that Russian President Vladimir Putin's invasion of Ukraine triggered a display of European and transatlantic cohesion that few could have anticipated before the war.[1] It has galvanised NATO, prompting it to add two new members, Finland and Sweden, one of which borders Russia and both of which stand to appreciably strengthen the Alliance.[2] So far, the EU has adopted, in close coordination with its partners, eight packages of sanctions, provided vast financial and military support to Ukraine, offered protection to millions of Ukrainians escaping from war and granted Ukraine candidate status in the EU.[3] Moreover, the EU is gradually working towards a common position to deal with the energy crisis. While falling short of a united stance on the question of whether to cap gas prices, the European Council meeting on 20 October 2022 made significant progress in this direction by agreeing to move forward on joint gas purchases, work towards establishing a new gas-price benchmark that better reflects the market, and decide on a temporary dynamic price corridor on natural-gas transactions that would limit price spikes.[4]

The second argument is based on an analogy with previous EU responses to crises, which have demonstrated the Union's resilience and its capacity to turn problems into opportunities and to advance European integration.[5] The most obvious example is the most recent: Europe's reaction to the COVID-19 pandemic. The economic and societal challenges associated with the pandemic were perhaps even more daunting than the ones Europe is now facing. Governments' radical measures to limit cross-border movements of goods and people within and across EU member states resulted in an unprecedented economic contraction in 2020, as the EU's real GDP fell by 6.1%, more than during the global financial crisis.[6]

Yet Europe managed this crisis with a display of political unity that many hailed as the materialisation of Europe's 'Hamiltonian moment'.[7] After years of resisting debt-mutualisation projects coming from 'southern' countries such as Italy and France, Germany acknowledged that 'exceptional events call for exceptional new methods' and in May 2020 gave the green light to the adoption of a massive €750 billion stimulus package (€360bn for loans and €390bn for subsidies) to be financed through collectively pooled debt obligations. In the event, the COVID-19 pandemic, with its massive health and socio-economic implications, proved an opportunity to move forward in terms of integration, ultimately stimulating EU member states to strengthen Europe.

Could the Ukraine crisis produce another display of European unity? Nathalie Tocci recently put forth a 'more pain, more gain' argument: the more acute Putin's external threat, the more unifying its effect on Europe and the higher the likelihood that European leaders would be able to adapt, react and bounce back.[8] From a normative standpoint, this argument is unobjectionable, even inspiring. A stronger Europe emerging from the Ukraine crisis is a desirable outcome not only for Europeans, but also for those who believe that a united and cohesive Europe is a precondition for an international order that has appeared elusive.[9] Analytically, however, there are several reasons for scepticism about Europe's ability to replicate the COVID success story.

Asymmetrical effects

The economic consequences of this crisis are more asymmetrically distributed across the member states than those of the pandemic. Of course, the pandemic too hit different member states in different ways and to different degrees. Divergences in fiscal capacity between northern and southern member states affected decisions about social-spending strategies to cope with the economic downturn. But the health challenges, measures of social containment, and magnitude and speed of economic collapse were largely the same across EU member states. The fact that the consequences of that exogenous shock were roughly symmetrically distributed among different member states was key to an efficient collective response. All governments could clearly see both that there was no unilateral way out of the crisis and that the collective gains stemming from cooperation in the form of a debt mutualisation would be large and uniformly distributed. As game-theoretical models of international cooperation – in particular, the Prisoner's Dilemma – suggest, this is precisely the kind of constellation of actors' interests that facilitates cooperation: for all governments the potential gains deriving from unilateral, non-cooperative strategies were small or non-existent, while the gains from cooperative behaviour were large and obvious.[10]

The consequences of the current crisis, however, are more asymmetrically distributed, making cooperative strategies less attractive to all member states. For one, not all member states are equally affected by the energy crisis, because not all of them are high-energy-consuming countries. Countries where industrial production comprises a relatively large share of domestic GDP, such as France, Germany and Italy, are generally more vulnerable to disruptions of energy markets than countries whose economies have become more service-based, such as Belgium or the Netherlands. Furthermore, cleavages exist between industrial producers, with Germany and Italy being much more heavily dependent on Russian gas than France due to the latter's heavy reliance on domestically produced nuclear energy. As noted, EU member states also have varying fiscal capabilities for addressing the economic challenges caused by the spike of energy prices. Germany's unilateral decision to adopt a massive €200bn gas-price-relief fund contrasts starkly with Italy's meagre fiscal measures to contain domestic energy prices. An east–west divide has also emerged on the severity of Russia's threat to the European security order. Such cross-cutting cleavages make cooperative solutions more difficult to achieve, creating stronger incentives for unilateral action and making it harder to define a collective response acceptable to all.

A weakened stabiliser

As Charles Kindleberger famously argued, international cooperation is greatly facilitated by the presence of a stabiliser – that is, a country both able and willing to provide public goods, discourage free-riding and support collective action.[11] Germany played such role in the COVID-19 crisis, shifting from being a staunch opponent of debt mutualisation to a driving force behind the pandemic-recovery fund. Without Germany's support, there would have been no recovery plan and no success story. European solidarity materialised because German chancellor Angela Merkel decided it was worth transferring about €65bn in German tax revenue to other EU countries to save Europe.

Several factors suggest that Germany might not fully assume this responsibility with respect to the Ukraine crisis. Germany's economy entered a downward spiral as price hikes for electricity and gas reduced the purchasing power of private households and led to a decline in private consumer spending. As a result, the German economy is expected to lapse into recession, with its GDP estimated to decline by 0.7% in 2023.[12] German industry's manufacturing output — which accounts for more than one-fifth of the country's GDP – is estimated to have dropped by 2.5% in 2022, and is predicted to diminish by about 5% in 2023, according to Deutsche Bank.[13] Driving the downward spiral are skyrocketing energy prices. They have risen nearly 400% in 2022, prompting some to consider that this is 'the starting point for an accelerated deindustrialization in Germany'.[14] Obviously, rising energy prices have hit energy-intensive industries, such as chemical, glass and metal producers, and, critically, the automobile industry. The latter could experience a permanent shift. Some 85% of the officers of automobile manufacturers and automotive suppliers surveyed by Germany's automotive-industry association view the country as an uncompetitive location because of high energy prices and insecure supply, while 22% would consider moving production abroad.[15]

The Ukraine crisis places at risk Germany's model of industrial production. Since the 1990s, German producers have relied on a steady flow of inexpensive natural gas from Russia to fuel their factories. This source of cheap energy is likely to be absent for the foreseeable future. Indeed, EU–Russia relations probably would not be normalised even in the case of a negotiated end to the war. A country with such bleak medium- to long-term economic prospects is unlikely to be willing to take up additional burdens to help European partners and act as a stabiliser. German leaders could instead feel compelled to unilaterally secure the country's relative position within Europe's economy. Indicators include Germany's unilateral decision to adopt a €200bn energy package, as well as its resistance to an EU-wide mechanism to enforce a price cap on natural-gas imports and to proposals for energy-related joint EU debt issuance.

Populist nationalism

Nationalist, populist and anti-European parties across Europe are key challenges for the long-term stability of European integration, and such parties usually thrive when socio-economic conditions dramatically worsen.[16] The current crisis has much greater potential than the pandemic did to stimulate support for these parties. As time passed, it became increasingly clear that the global nature of the pandemic could not be effectively tackled with merely national solutions, but required cooperation among states. This strategic interdependence muted populist and nationalist rhetoric.[17] But the asymmetrical distributional consequences of the Ukraine crisis make those that are suffering the least and those suffering the most highly susceptible to such rhetoric.

In northern European countries with relatively sound budgets and high fiscal capacities, populists and nationalists are likely to champion the 'frugal north' against the 'profligate south'. In turn, southern European populists and nationalists would find it easier to marshal support against northern countries owing to the latter's perceived disregard for the south's struggles. Thus, strategic interdependence with respect to the Ukraine crisis only fuels populist and nationalist social grievances. The recent electoral successes of Jimmie Åkesson's Sverigedemokraterna in Sweden, Giorgia Meloni's Fratelli d'Italia in Italy, and Marine Le Pen's Rassemblement National in France are only the most visible indications of the crisis's potential to stimulate a populist and nationalist backlash across Europe.

Which peace?

EU member states shared views as to which fundamental goal they were pursuing when tackling the pandemic: developing and securing a vaccine that could be swiftly and widely distributed to the public with a view to restoring life as it was before as quickly as possible. As to the Ukraine crisis, while European governments share key objectives, such as reducing dependency on Russian gas and mitigating socio-economic disruptions, and have so far been able to maintain a united front in sanctioning Russia and supporting Ukraine, clear divisions are emerging concerning the terms of an acceptable peace.

There are two broad camps. Countries such as France, Germany and perhaps Italy are prone to espouse a minimalist definition of peace, which broadly entails restoring the status quo ante, defined as the situation prevailing immediately prior to 24 February 2022, the date of the Russian invasion. Whether Ukrainian territory should include Crimea remains an open question, but for later disposition at an unspecified time. Countries such as Poland and the Baltic states, which are more directly exposed to Russia, are more inclined to subscribe to a maximalist definition of peace that calls for a long-term eradication of Russia's threat and could logically imply regime change in Russia. Divisions on this issue are a potential source of tension that could spill into internal discussions about how to cope with the energy crisis and how to strengthen European foreign and security policy.

The time factor

Finally, in the case of the COVID-19 pandemic, time worked in favour of a cooperative European solution. The relatively even distribution of the crisis's costs across Europe's member states was key in this regard. As time passed, it became increasingly evident that opposition to cooperative solutions implied forgoing large collective gains. In this crisis, time works in the opposite direction. Distributional consequences are becoming even more varied. Accordingly, as the crisis's time horizon expands, EU member states' policy preferences are likely to diverge and become more difficult to reconcile. For instance, EU member states that suffer less from rising energy prices may come to realise that while their economies may have worsened overall, their relative positions within the EU's internal market may have strengthened.

In particular, Germany will be less likely to step up. Its role as regional stabiliser has depended on the capacity of its domestic capital markets to deliver low inflation and its domestic labour markets to provide skilled personnel. These assets enabled Germany to remain a competitive industrial producer in the face of China's rise as the world's main hub for industrial production, and thus to consistently run current-account surpluses that produced sound and balanced budgets. Long-term prospects of rising energy prices risk the acceleration of Germany's deindustrialisation and imperil its status as Europe's stabiliser.

The economic strain imposed by the crisis on European firms, households and governments is already substantial, and the first winter since the war began is far from over. The longer the crisis drags on, the more populists and nationalists are likely to be able to capitalise politically on popular discontent. Differences on the definition of an acceptable peace are also likely to deepen. Over time, EU member states facing relatively few economic challenges or overridingly determined to disempower Russia could intensify maximalist war aims, while those suffering the most increase pressure for compromise.

*   *   *

The tenuousness of Europe's resistance does not mean that Europe should leave Ukraine to its fate and seek swift accommodation with Putin. Such a scenario is not feasible because the decision rests primarily with Ukrainians, who are entitled to decide on the timing and content of any negotiated settlement, and with major powers such as the United States and China, which have economic and military resources that enable them to directly shape the arc of the war. It is not desirable because, to paraphrase Hedley Bull, considerations pertaining to the realm of order should not be disentangled from evaluations about justice.[18] For Europe to sacrifice the latter in the name of the former would probably strike an even more fatal blow to Europe's unity. If Europe is to remain united, however, it must seek a solution to the crisis that is both just and prompt. This requires avoiding the temptation of pursuing maximalist aims and a broader acceptance of a calibrated definition of peace calling for a restoration of Ukrainian territorial integrity immediately prior to Russia's February 2022 invasion.

Notes

[1] See, for example, Nigel Gould-Davies, 'Putin's Strategic Failure', *Survival*, vol. 64, no. 2, April–May 2022, pp. 7–16.

[2] See William Alberque and Benjamin Schreer, 'What Kind of Allies Will Finland and Sweden Be?', *Survival*, vol. 64, no. 6, December 2022–January 2023, pp. 123–36.

[3] See European Commission, 'Ukraine: EU Agrees on Eighth Package of Sanctions', Press Release, 6 October 2022, https://ec.europa.eu/commission/presscorner/detail/en/ip_22_5989.

[4] See European Council, 'European Council Conclusions', 21 October 2022, https://www.consilium.europa.

eu/media/59728/2022-10-2021-euco-conclusions-en.pdf.

5   See, for instance, Nathalie Tocci, 'Can Russia Divide Europe? Why a False Peace Could Be Worse than a Long War', *Foreign Affairs*, 5 August 2022, https://www.foreignaffairs.com/europe/can-russia-divide-europe.

6   Maarten Verwey and Alan Monks, 'The EU Economy After COVID-19: Implications for Economic Governance', Center for Economic Policy Research, 21 October 2021, https://cepr.org/voxeu/columns/eu-economy-after-covid-19-implications-economic-governance.

7   Christakis Georgiou, 'Europe's "Hamiltonian Moment"? On the Political Uses and Explanatory Usefulness of a Recurrent Historical Comparison', *Economy and Society*, vol. 51, no. 1, November 2021, pp. 138–59.

8   See Tocci, 'Can Russia Divide Europe?'.

9   See Arlo Poletti, Lorenzo Zambernardi and Dirk De Bièvre, 'Time for a New Atlanticism: The EU–China Comprehensive Agreement on Investment and the International Order', *International Spectator*, November 2022.

10 See Duncan Snidal, 'Coordination Versus Prisoners' Dilemma: Implications for International Cooperation and Regimes', *American Political Science Review,* vol. 79, no. 4, December 1985, pp. 923–42.

11 See Charles P. Kindleberger, 'Dominance and Leadership in the International Economy: Exploitation, Public Goods, and Free Rides', *International Studies Quarterly*, vol. 25, no. 2, June 1981, pp. 242–54.

12 IFO Institute, 'Joint Economic Forecast Autumn 2022: Energy Crisis: Inflation, Recession, Welfare Loss', 29 September 2022, https://www.ifo.de/en/facts/2022-09-29/joint-economic-forecast-autumn-2022-energy-crisis-inflation-recession-welfare-loss.

13 Deutsche Bank Research, 'German Economy: Out in the Cold', 27 September 2022, https://www.dbresearch.com/PROD/RPS_EN-PROD/PROD0000000000524797/German_economy%3A_Out_in_the_cold.PDF?undefined&realload=~Nwf5Dpvrxix4Qrvm KSpcZWGoaYkEWynIL7JaJ~j/IG1Z3s3wUNvEOXTAAjjICQH.

14 Anna Cooban, 'Rocketing Energy Costs Are Savaging German Industry', CNN Business, 28 October 2022, https://edition.cnn.com/2022/10/07/energy/german-industry-energy-prices/index.html.

15 Verband der Automobilindustrie, 'Energy Prices and Security of Supply: Germany Lacks Competitiveness', Press Release, 13 September 2022, https://www.vda.de/en/press/press-releases/2022/220913_PM_Energy-prices-and-security-of-supply_Germany-lacks-competitiveness.

16 See Italo Colantone and Piero Stanig, 'The Trade Origins of Economic Nationalism: Import Competition and Voting Behavior in Western Europe', *American Journal of Political Science*, vol. 62, no. 4, October 2018, pp. 936–53; and Helen V. Milner, 'Voting for Populism in Europe: Globalization, Technological Change, and the Extreme Right', *Comparative Political Studies*, vol. 54, no. 13, 2021, pp. 2,286–320.

[17] See Bengt Johansson, David Nicolas Hopmann and Adam Shehata, 'When the Rally-around-the-flag Effect Disappears, or: When the COVID-19 Pandemic Becomes "Normalized"', *Journal of Elections, Public Opinion and Parties*, vol. 31, supplement 1, June 2021, pp. 321–34.

[18] See Hedley Bull, *The Anarchical Society: A Study of Order in World Politics*, 4th edition (New York: Columbia University Press, 2012).

Calibrating the EU's Trade Dependency

Agnieszka Gehringer

The European Union's commitment to free trade among its members and with non-EU countries and regions has shaped its external policy. One of its driving assumptions has been that the EU's market power in the international system would afford it the ability to extend its unique model of capitalist development to less developed and less market-oriented trading partners. This strategy faced a bitter reality check first with the COVID-19 pandemic and then, to an even greater extent, with the Russian invasion of Ukraine. The pandemic led to severe disruptions in economic activity, resulting in weaknesses along some important value and supply chains, especially in the food and health sectors. The energy crisis triggered by the war in Ukraine reinforced the perception that an uncontrolled expansion of trade relations may lead to undesirable external dependencies.

On 27 February 2022, three days after the Russian invasion of Ukraine, German Chancellor Olaf Scholz announced a radical shift in the core elements of German foreign and security policy whereby soft power would become subordinate to deterrence backed by military strength.[1] Risks stemming from strategic dependencies are sharply perceived elsewhere, too. In November 2022, for example, the Canadian Ministry of Innovation, Science and Economic Development ordered three Chinese groups to sell

Agnieszka Gehringer is a professor of economics at the Cologne University of Applied Sciences and a senior research analyst at the Flossbach von Storch Research Institute.

Survival | vol. 65 no. 1 | February–March 2023 | pp. 81–96   https://doi.org/10.1080/00396338.2023.2172855

their stakes in three domestic lithium-mining companies based on findings from a defence and intelligence review implying that such investments weakened national security.[2] In 2021, the EU published an update to its new industrial strategy based on the need to 'strengthen Europe's open strategic autonomy and the new partnership approach with industry and like-minded international partners'.[3]

Trade dependencies are not bad per se. The ability to exchange commodities, products, services and knowledge across borders yields efficiency gains due to cost savings and qualitative improvements.[4] Free international trade and concomitant trade dependencies can be beneficial in some sensitive areas – including national defence – if imported materials, equipment and technology cost less or are of better quality than domestic alternatives. However, trade can also degrade a country's national security when, for instance, its source for a mission-critical product or service is a dominant global supplier of that product or service whose national interests diverge from those of the importing country.

This article maps trade dependencies, with a particular focus on strategic imports, and draws heavily on the established economic analysis of free trade versus protectionism. One of the more widely shared views in this field is that free trade – by minimising efficiency losses from protectionism – can help raise living standards.[5] But the literature also elaborates valid arguments for deviating from free trade. Moreover, new analyses of trade in non-competitive markets have yielded arguments for trade intervention on the basis of 'strategic trade policy'.[6] Strategic trade policy calls for limits on free trade if it produces dependencies that jeopardise national security.[7] This work has examined mainly the national-security consequences of US dependence on strategic resources, especially oil, and has largely ignored the EU.[8]

Conceptualising and measuring strategic trade dependence

Economic dependence implies reliance in production or consumption on a few suppliers of goods, services or other resources. It can be domestic or external. In the latter case, dependence means that an economic system is conditioned by the development and performance of another economy. Trade dependencies imply concentrations of imports on a few external sources and exports on a limited number of foreign destinations. External dependencies can be driven by the stake ownership of domestic investors in foreign companies or foreign investors in domestic companies. Flows of labour, skills, knowledge and technology can also be sources of external dependencies. This article, however, focuses on trade flows as a driver of dependence.

Existing or potential trade dependencies can constitute both risks and opportunities. On the export side, high foreign demand might be a sign of strong competitive advantages for domestic suppliers and thus an opportunity to gain additional revenues. At the same time, unexpected demand shocks or undesirable developments within international financial markets might undermine foreign demand as a secure source of revenues to exporters. Moreover, dependence on primary commodity exports – the so-called resource curse – is likely to have negative economic consequences in terms of high price volatility and low productivity growth.

On the import side, dependence on foreign suppliers might reflect an efficient division of labour, resulting from cost-reducing outsourcing decisions. Moreover, purchasing goods from abroad could lower output volatility by reducing exposure to domestic shocks. However, reliance on imports could be risky, as when country-level shocks affect a specific exporter. Openness to trade also increases specialisation and thus may lead to higher GDP volatility. Moreover, dependence on imports might jeopardise corporate strategies and economic competitiveness in both the short term and the long term if economic activities with high value-added and innovation features are systematically relocated abroad.[9]

While trade openness and the resulting dependencies – especially on the import side – are in principle desirable, they can damage national security if they lead to strategic dependency. This will occur if the importing country's reliance on a strategically critical product from the exporting country enables that country to substantially control the availability of that product to the importing country.

Since the determination of strategic goals is particular to governments and evolves with changing socio-economic and technological circumstances, no fixed list of strategically critical sectors or products is possible.[10]

Accordingly, the eventual determination of strategic dependencies requires a detailed assessment of specific current and future priorities. Nevertheless, a firm consensus has developed that the core goals across economic systems – at least developed ones – relate to internal and external security, safety and health.[11] The commodities, products, equipment, skills, assets, facilities, networks and systems that are essential to the achievement of such core goals constitute critical infrastructure.

Strategic dependencies arise through a non-negligible reliance of critical infrastructure on resources originating from abroad or supplied by foreign-owned entities. During a pandemic or a geopolitical crisis, strategic dependencies may lead to a national emergency.[12] Although there is no model-based framework, the consensus view suggests that reliance on foreign supply rises to the level of strategic dependency when three conditions are satisfied: 1) a country or region is a net importer of a good; 2) the country or region receives more than 50% of its total imports of the good from a single partner; and 3) the partner in question possesses at least 30% of the global trade share for the good. Thus, under strategic dependency, the exporter is a dominant player in the global market, and it is difficult for the importing country or region in question to readily obtain the product elsewhere.

Alternative approaches have been used for identifying strategic import dependencies from China. Derek Scissors's framework is based on two main 'parameters'. Firstly, net imports of a good constitute a substantial portion of domestic consumption. Secondly, these imports are at risk because they come from an unreliable source or their supply lines are vulnerable.[13] Although these criteria are straightforward and transparent, a country's relative importance in consumption might lead to a misleading assessment of the overall importance of the product in question. Even goods whose domestic consumption is small – such as rare-earth minerals – could be economically or strategically vital. Furthermore, the focus on current consumption underplays the potential for future changes in consumption patterns.

Another noteworthy approach is the bottom-up one followed by the European Commission, and based on a step-by-step procedure. The first step involves identifying traded products for which the EU is most dependent on foreign sources. Within that category, dependence is determined according to three Core Dependency Indicators (CDIs) to which certain thresholds apply.[14] CDI_1 measures the concentration of EU imports from extra-EU sources, CDI_2 quantifies the importance of extra-EU imports in total external (EU and non-EU) demand, and CDI_3 reflects the substitutability of extra-EU imports with EU production. In the second step, particular trade dependencies are linked to the most sensitive ecosystems. The final step involves qualitatively assessing specific strategic dependencies.

The latter approach corresponds to the one applied in this article. CDI_1, measuring import concentration, closely relates to the second criterion of requiring that more than 50% of imports originate from one country. That criterion, however, offers a more precise indication of concentration and is also more conservative than CDI_1, imposing the requirement that more than 50% of imports should come from a single source compared with 40% for CDI_1.[15] CDI_3, regarding import substitutability, tracks with the first requirement of being a net importer of a good. Insofar as CDI_2 indicates the relative importance of non-EU suppliers, it should be interpreted more as a measure of import concentration than one of substitutability of imports with domestic production.

Mapping the EU's trade dependencies

Currently, almost 23% of the EU's total imports come from China, followed by 11% from the United States and around 8% from Russia. Some 18% of the EU's total exports go to the US, followed by 13% to the United Kingdom and 10% to China (see Figure 1).

Whereas the EU's trade dependence on Russia has diminished somewhat since Russia's annexation of Crimea in early 2014, trade links with China have increased on both the export and import side (see Figure 2).

Russia's invasion of Ukraine and the resulting energy crisis have demonstrated that close trade relations with authoritarian regimes weaken national security. This concern logically extends to China, whose industrial policy seeks to reinforce China's global economic dominance.[16] In fact, given that China is far more important than Russia or other trading partners to

Figure 1: **Country-specific import and export shares in the EU27, 2021**

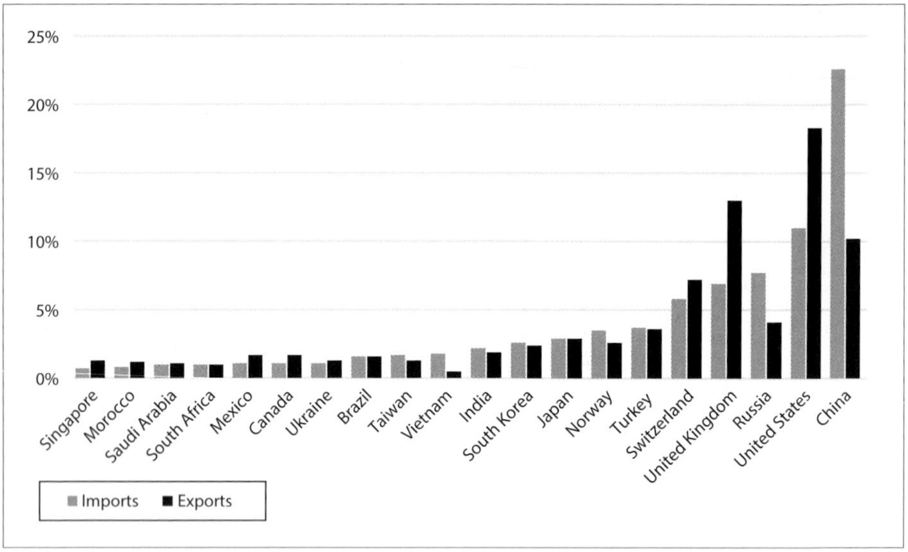

Sources: Eurostat and Comtrade databases

EU trade, China has greater power to interfere significantly in intra-EU economic activities. Political trends do not appear to ameliorate this problem.
Contrary to early post-Cold War hopes and expectations, close trade relations with authoritarian regimes have not precipitated significant shifts
towards democracy.

Among the largest EU economies, Germany has the strongest trade links
with China in terms of both imports and exports. The bilateral trade relationship has intensified significantly over the last two decades, rising from
3.4% to 11.9% for German imports from China and from 1.6% to 7.6% for
German exports to China. France, Italy and Spain have increased their trade
relations as well. In particular, Spain's import dependency grew from 2.8%
in 2000 to almost 10% in 2021. Spain's export dependency increased from
0.4% in 2000 to 2.6% in 2021, France's from 1% to almost 5% over the same
period. However, France has managed to reduce its import dependency
from 9.2% in 2015 to 6.7% in 2021 (see Figure 3).

Across the broad product groups, based on the one-digit codes of the
Standard International Trade Classification (SITC), the strongest EU foreign-
trade relations are for machinery and transport equipment.[17] In 2021, the

Figure 2: **EU27 imports/exports from/to Russia and China as shares of total EU imports/exports**

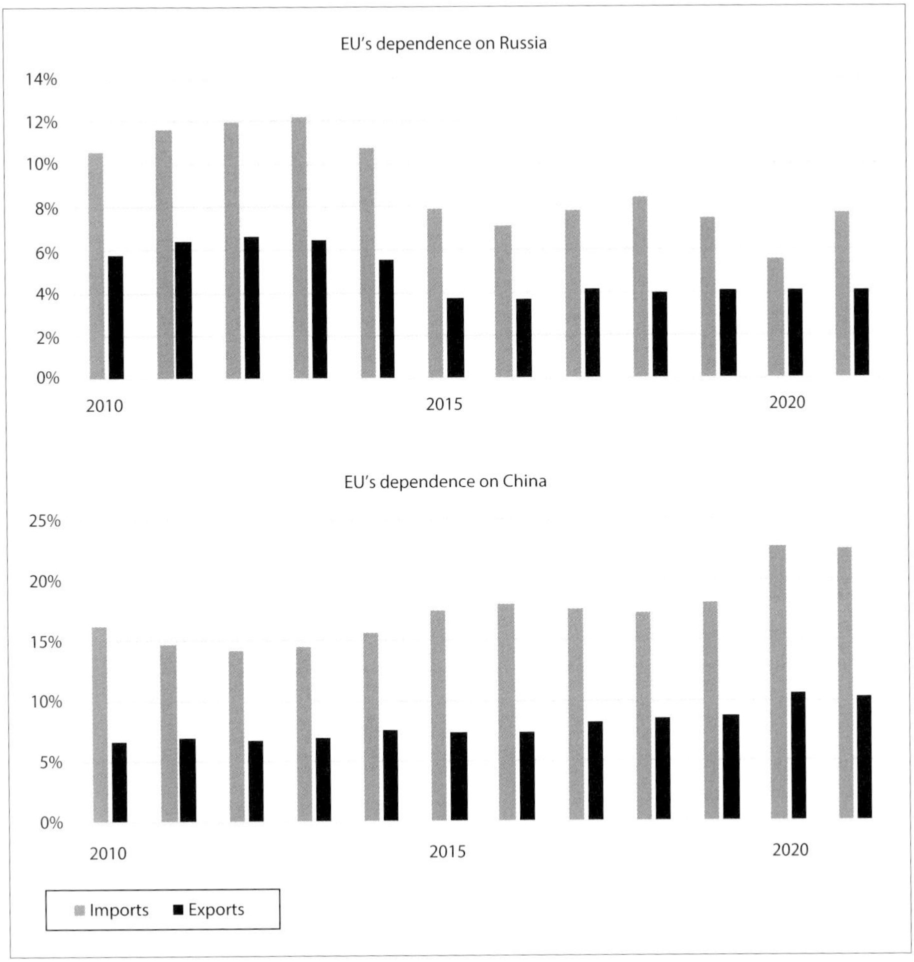

Sources: Eurostat and Comtrade databases

import share in this product group over EU-wide imports increased from 29% in 2010 to 32% in 2021 (see Figure 4). The export share declined from 42% in 2010 to 38% in 2021 (see Figure 5).

The second-strongest trade dependency arises in the miscellaneous category of other manufactured goods, which includes a range of final-consumption goods such as furniture, clothing, footwear and accessories; sophisticated products such as scientific instruments, photo apparatus, optical goods, watches and clocks; and arms and ammunition.

Figure 3: **Trade dependence on China (shares of imports from and exports to China over total imports/exports) in the largest EU member states**

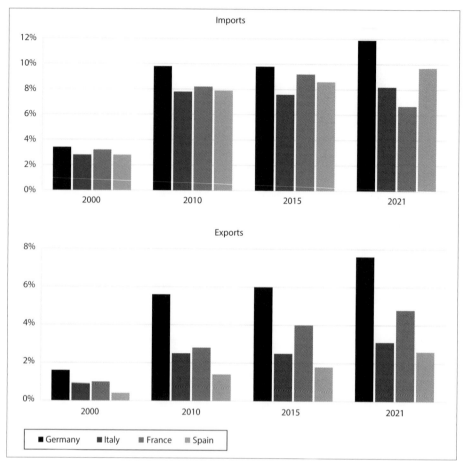

Sources: Eurostat and Comtrade databases

For imports, a remarkable dependence emerges for mineral fuels, lubricants and related materials, as well as chemicals and related products. Both categories include important intermediate goods used in various industrial production processes. The EU is also highly dependent on exports of chemicals and related products, less so on exports of mineral fuels, lubricants and related materials (see Figure 5).

Finally, for imports of almost all the product categories displayed in Figure 4, China plays a dominant role, reflecting the country's rise as a manufacturing superpower since the 1970s.

Figure 4: **EU's imports across the product groups, as a share of total imports**

Source: Eurostat database

Figure 5: **EU's exports across the product groups, as a share of total exports**

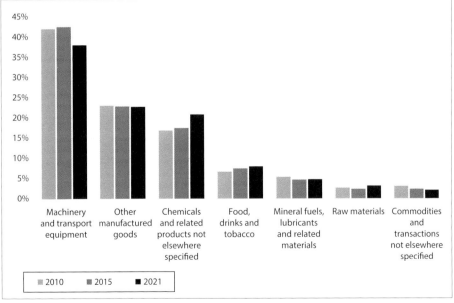

Source: Eurostat database

A granular view of EU import dependency

Tables 1 and 2 summarise the EU's strategic import dependencies on China for the main categories of final-consumption and intermediate goods as of 2021. These are six-digit Harmonised System (HS) categories, for which all three conditions for strategic import dependency are satisfied.[18] The second column shows the EU's overall import values for the respective product categories. The third column indicates the shares of EU imports from China as a percentage of the EU total in each category. The fourth column shows China's global market shares in terms of global trade flows. The last column gives the values of export–import balances. Bold entries in the third and fourth columns indicate particularly strong strategic dependencies, with an over 75% share of EU imports from China and over 50% of global market share captured by China.

Among the top ten consumer goods, a very strong import dependency exists for popular electronic devices. It is significant on account of the high value of overall EU imports in this category. In 2021, more than 70% of

Table 1: **EU's strategic dependence on imports from China for selected final-consumption-good categories, classified according to the descending value of overall EU imports of the goods, 2021**

HS category	Overall EU imports of the good (in US$ millions)	EU import dependence on China	China's global market share	EU trade balance (in US$ millions)
1. Telephones for cellular or wireless networks	43,185	71.1%	**55.5%**	-25,264
2. Automatic data-processing machines	40,951	**93.4%**	**72.6%**	-36,772
3. Communication apparatus (excl. telephone sets or base stations)	33,298	55.2%	31.0%	-16,696
4. Photosensitive electrical apparatus, incl. photovoltaic	13,235	**82.6%**	48.5%	-10,910
5. Electrical static converters	12,511	60.8%	35.0%	-2,744
6. Tricycles, scooters, pedal cars and similar wheeled toys	8,351	**82.8%**	**67.2%**	-5,531
7. Games, video-game consoles	5,793	**75.5%**	**55.9%**	-4,700
8. Non-sport footwear	3,840	58.1%	**55.4%**	-1,572
9. Combined refrigerator–freezers	2,380	63.6%	30.3%	-1,577
10. Microwave ovens of a kind used for domestic purposes	909	**80.5%**	**70.1%**	-789

The reported good categories have the following HS codes: 1 = 851712, 2 = 847130, 3 = 851762, 4 = 854140, 5 = 850440, 6 = 950300, 7 = 950450, 8 = 640419, 9 = 841810, 10 = 851650
Source: Comtrade database

EU imports of mobile phones originated from China, and China enjoyed a global market share of almost 56%. Similarly, the EU imports 93% of its automatic data-processing machines and 80.5% of its microwave ovens from China, which commands 70% of the global market share for each category of product. Also, 82.8% of the EU's wheeled toys and 76% of its video games come from China. Cutting off these imports, of course, is unlikely to have strategic consequences (see Table 1).

Even more critical are strategic dependencies on intermediate goods. The unavailability of an essential component has the potential to disrupt industrial

Table 2: **EU's strategic dependence on imports from China for selected intermediate-good categories, classified according to the descending value of overall EU imports of the goods, 2021**

HS category	Overall EU imports of the good (in US$ millions)	EU import dependence on China	China's global market share	EU trade balance (in US$ millions)
1. Electric motors and generators, DC of an output not exceeding 750 W	2,211.4	54.0%	27.6%	-725.7
2. Printed circuit boards	6,117	67.2%	35.8%	-4,944
3. Permanent magnets and metal articles intended to become permanent magnets	1,054	**85.5%**	**64.0%**	-923.7
4. Locks of base metal other than those for motor vehicles or furniture	533.8	55.4%	37.4%	-73.6
5. Cells and batteries, primary manganese dioxide	517.7	**84.9%**	48.1%	-328.9
6. Safety glass	514.8	59.5%	**61.0%**	-365.3
7. Magnesium unwrought containing less than 99.8% by weight of magnesium	175.6	**94.3%**	**69.9%**	-130.6
8. Rubber accelerators, prepared	73.2	64.8%	**55.9%**	-17.3
9. Vitamin B6 and its derivatives	65.4	**98.6%**	**68.6%**	-18.4
10. Chloramphenicol and its derivatives	32.9	**98.6%**	**90.2%**	-30.8
11. Manganese dioxide	26.5	70.3%	**57.3%**	-23.2
12. Heterocyclic compounds containing an unfused imidazole ring	23.7	54.9%	36.2%	-13.1
13. Reciprocating piston engines	13.1	**97.0%**	**76.0%**	-12.9
14. Hydroxides and peroxides of strontium or barium	6.6	**93.7%**	**69.5%**	-1.1
15. Rare-earth metals	4.0	**75.5%**	**58.8%**	-3.5

The reported good categories have the following HS codes: 1 = 850131, 2 = 853400, 3 = 850511, 4 = 830140, 5 = 850610, 6 = 700719, 7 = 810419, 8 = 381210, 9 = 293625, 10 = 294140, 11 = 282010, 12 = 293321, 13 = 840731, 14 = 281640, 15 = 280530
Source: Comtrade database

production both directly and indirectly, along supply and value chains, especially if alternative suppliers cannot be easily and quickly found. The EU is acutely dependent on China in several categories of electrical equipment and their spare parts, mechanical appliances, base metals and glass, as well as in certain categories of organic and inorganic chemicals (see Table 2). Although these products are often technologically less sophisticated, many of them are critical inputs in upstream production. Dependencies thus make entire industrial processes vulnerable to shocks. For instance, the EU's green-energy industry – especially the wind-energy sector – is highly dependent on China's supply of magnetic metals essential for wind turbines and modern electric motors. Also, minerals that power electric-car batteries are typically mined and refined by Chinese companies.

The last entry in Table 2 warrants special notice. Even if the nominal import value of rare-earth minerals is negligible and production data would superficially indicate little vulnerability, the category is crucial for industrial production, and specifically for the manufacturing of computers and core defence equipment.

Policy implications

In the context of increasing geopolitical tensions, the EU's growing economic dependence – especially on China – suggests a prospective loss of strategic autonomy. China has already shown in the past that it is willing to use its market control over crucial resources to effectively blackmail trading partners. In 2009, China suspended its export of rare-earth minerals that were crucial for computer manufacturing and the production of military goods. Under the increasingly authoritarian leadership of Xi Jinping, such behaviour will most likely recur and intensify.[19]

It appears likely that the communist leadership will continue to advance two industrial-policy campaigns – 'Made in China 2025' and 'China Standards 2035' – with an eye to consolidating China's global economic leadership. The first campaign, launched in 2013, is aimed at securing a controlling position along major global supply chains through research and development efforts by Chinese state-owned enterprises and technological advances.[20] With the second strategy, the Chinese government aims to gain sway over international commercial standards and thereby set the terms of the global industrial order, including in the digital space.[21]

Understanding underlying dependencies and reducing those that portend the EU's strategic vulnerability should be a main priority of the EU's industrial policy. The EU has already launched appropriately targeted initiatives, but additional concrete steps are required.[22] Eliminating all possible vulnerabilities is, of course, unfeasible. But a coherent and systematic assessment of existing external dependencies is critical to protecting Europe's strategic autonomy while also preserving a versatile and diversified trade policy.

This article is an initial attempt at such an assessment. A more comprehensive and thorough baseline analysis and regular updates are needed.[23] However, the data required for an enhanced assessment is often unavailable or incomplete. Although HS product categories at the six-digit level are already very detailed, they are not always granular enough to monitor dependencies for specific products or materials. Moreover, detailed production and consumption data for each EU member state, collected according to the HS classification, would significantly enrich the investigatory framework.

Economic policy reforms should aim primarily to encourage businesses to adopt practices that will diversify the EU's trade relations in areas of current or potential strategic dependency. One measure might be to abolish or at least substantially reduce investment guarantees for business activities in and with China. Another would be to reduce intra-EU regulatory and broader institutional barriers that discourage domestic businesses from innovating. Still another effective strategy would be to develop new export and import markets through intergovernmental agreements that break down existing trade barriers and create incentives for investment in alternative trade partners.

*   *   *

In the short term, the EU could lose efficiency and profits in reducing its dependency on China. In the longer term, however, diversification should pay off as new capacities yield economies of scale and scope. The EU has missed some opportunities along these lines by overemphasising high standards of environmental and social sustainability to the detriment of diversification. Such a strategy poses undue risks to the EU's strategic autonomy and geopolitical influence, which are essential to winning more rigorous compliance with those very standards.

Notes

1   See Bernhard Blumenau, 'Breaking with Convention? *Zeitenwende* and the Traditional Pillars of German Foreign Policy', *International Affairs*, vol. 98, no. 6, November 2022, pp. 1,895–913.

2   For more details, see Government of Canada, 'Government of Canada Orders the Divestiture of Investments by Foreign Companies in Canadian Critical Minerals Companies', 2 November 2022, https://www.canada.ca/en/innovation-science-economic-development/news/2022/10/government-of-canada-orders-the-divestiture-of-investments-by-foreign-companies-in-canadian-critical-mineral-companies.html.

3   European Commission, 'Updating the 2020 New Industrial Strategy: Building a Stronger Single Market for Europe's Recovery', Communication from the Commission to the European Parliament, the Council, the European Economic and Social Committee and the Committee of the Regions, 5 May 2021, p. 3, https://commission.europa.eu/system/files/2021-05/communication-industrial-strategy-update-2020_en.pdf.

4   There is a rich and extensive literature on the link between trade liberalisation and efficiency gains, covering the different aspects and channels through which trade fuels positive effects on welfare.

5   See, for example, Giancarlo Gandolfo, *Elements of International Economics* (Heidelberg: Springer Science & Business Media, 2004); and Paul R. Krugman, 'Is Free Trade Passé?', *Journal of Economic Perspectives*, vol. 1, no. 2, Fall 1987, pp. 131–44.

6   See, for instance, Barbara Spencer and James A. Brander, 'Strategic Trade Policy', in Steven N. Durlauf and Lawrence E. Blume (eds), *The New Palgrave Dictionary of Economics* (Basingstoke: Palgrave Macmillan, 2018).

7   See John Gerard Ruggie, 'International Regimes, Transactions, and Change: Embedded Liberalism in the Postwar Economic Order', *International Organization*, vol. 36, no. 2, Spring 1982, pp. 379–415. The argument plausibly dates back to Adam Smith's *An Inquiry into the Nature and Causes of the Wealth of Nations*, first published in 1776, in which he explained that one of the 'two cases in which it will generally be advantageous to lay some burden upon foreign trade for the encouragement of domestic industry' is 'when some particular sort of industry is necessary for the defence of the country'. Adam Smith, *The Wealth of Nations* (New York: Modern Library, 1937), p. 369.

8   At least since the mid-2010s, the trend towards intensifying national-security reviews can be observed in several Western countries, including Australia, Canada, Japan, New Zealand, the United Kingdom and

some EU member countries. For example, Australia adopted the Foreign Influence Transparency Scheme in 2018, New Zealand announced a ban on foreign political donations in December 2019, and in late 2022 Germany initiated efforts to reduce state investment in and export guarantees for German companies operating in China.

9   See Max J. Zenglein, 'Mapping and Recalibrating Europe's Economic Interdependence with China', *MERICS China Monitor*, 18 November 2020, https://merics.org/sites/default/files/2020-11/Merics%20ChinaMonitor_Mapping%20and%20recalibrating%20(1).pdf.

10   The set of industrial goods or services regarded as strategically important evolved from iron, steam engines and shipbuilding in the eighteenth and nineteenth centuries, through more capital-intensive and sophisticated goods from the chemical and pharmaceutical industry in the twentieth century, to data- and information-intensive products in the twenty-first century.

11   See, for example, European Commission, 'Updating the 2020 New Industrial Strategy'. The United Nations' Sustainable Development Goals framework is built around the concepts of security (internal, external and international) and health (physical, mental, environmental).

12   This was the experience of the United Kingdom in the early twentieth century, as the country saw its position weakening against Germany, which became globally dominant in the production of synthetic dyes. For these

the UK was so dependent on Germany that during the early months of the First World War the country continued secretly importing German dyes.

13   See Derek Scissors, 'Free Markets and National Defense: U.S. Import Dependence on China', Backgrounder no. 2469, Heritage Foundation, 21 September 2010, https://thf_media.s3.amazonaws.com/2010/pdf/bg2469.pdf.

14   The applied thresholds are as follows: $CDI_1 > 0.4$, $CDI_2 > 0.5$, $CDI_3 > 1$.

15   CDI_1 is a Herfindahl–Hirschman Index, varying between 0 (no concentration) and 1 (maximum concentration). For example, a value of $CDI_1 = 0.4$ implies that 40% of imports are concentrated in one or a few countries.

16   See Agnieszka Gehringer and Norbert F. Tofall, 'Modernisierung in der Volksrepublik China: Strukturwandel und Wirtschaftswachstum ohne politisch-gesellschaftliche Freiheit?' [Modernisation in the People's Republic of China: structural change and economic growth without political and social freedom?], Flossbach von Storch Research Institute, Makroanalyse, 15 September 2016, https://www.flossbachvonstorch-researchinstitute.com/fileadmin/user_upload/RI/Studien/files/studie-160915-modernisierung-in-der-vr-china.pdf.

17   SITC is correlated with the subheadings of the Harmonised System classification.

18   The Harmonised System is a global product-classification system devised and administered by the World Customs Organization and updated every five years. It serves as the foundation for import- and export-

classification systems used by most trading nations. It is organised into 21 sections, subdivided into 99 chapters (two-digit), 1,244 headings (four-digit) and 5,224 subheadings (six-digit). There exist more detailed classifications, for instance, the Combined Nomenclature used by the EU member states, which includes around 9,500 eight-digit codes, defined to meet specific EU needs. However, at this disaggregation level, there is no classification with sufficient correspondence covering trade flows in non-EU countries. The six-digit HS codes offer the most detailed disaggregation to analyse trade flows that are comparable across countries. The UN Comtrade database is an excellent source of this data, but it covers only trade in goods. Although the economic importance of service trade has grown, it still accounts for a relatively small share – 22.6% in 2020, according to the United Nations Conference on Trade and Development – of the world's total trade.

[19] See, for example, Gehringer and Tofall, 'Modernisierung in der Volksrepublik China'.

[20] See Max J. Zenglein and Anna Holzmann, 'Evolving Made in China 2025: China's Industrial Policy in the Quest for Global Tech Leadership', *MERICS Papers on China*, no. 8, July 2019, https://merics.org/sites/default/files/2020-04/MPOC_8_MadeinChina_2025_final_3.pdf.

[21] See Stacie Hoffmann, Dominique Lazanski and Emily Taylor, 'Standardising the Splinternet: How China's Technical Standards Could Fragment the Internet', *Journal of Cyber Policy*, vol. 5, no. 2, August 2020, pp. 239–64; and John Seaman, 'China and the New Geopolitics of Technical Standardization', *Notes de l'Ifri*, French Institute of International Relations, 27 January 2020, pp. 20–1, https://www.ifri.org/sites/default/files/atoms/files/seaman_china_standardization_2020.pdf. These rules have not always been based on fair treatment of commercial partners or rivals, and intellectual-property theft has slipped through the cracks, as shown by the theft of DuPont's trade secrets regarding the manufacture of 'brilliant white' dyes and the sale of those secrets to China's Pangang Group.

[22] There have been some promising developments along these lines. In 2019, the EU adopted a foreign-direct-investment screening regulation. The European Commission established an overview list of the raw materials that are considered most important economically and that carry a high supply risk, elaborating an action plan on economic and technological synergies between civil, defence and space industries.

[23] This analysis concentrates on imported goods, but its methodology could be extended to all cross-border transactions, including the exchange of services, capital, labour and technology.

Kindred Crises? Cuba 1962, Ukraine 2022

Jean-Yves Haine

On 6 October 2022, United States President Joe Biden stated publicly that 'for the first time since the Cuban Missile Crisis, we have a direct threat of the use of nuclear weapons, if in fact things continue down the path they'd been going. We have not faced the prospect of Armageddon since Kennedy and the Cuban Missile Crisis.' That crisis had arisen 60 years earlier, in October 1962, when the Soviet Union placed nuclear missiles in Cuba, less than 160 kilometres from the US mainland. He added that Russian President Vladimir Putin had not been 'joking' when he talked about using tactical nuclear, biological or chemical weapons because 'his military is, you might say, significantly underperforming'.[1]

Others echoed the president's concerns. Rose Gottemoeller, a former top US nuclear policymaker and NATO's deputy secretary general until 2019, told the BBC that Putin was unpredictable and that he might choose 'to use weapons of mass destruction, a single strike over the Black Sea, or perhaps a strike at a Ukrainian military facility to strike terror not only into the hearts of the Ukrainians but also its allies'.[2] Sam Nunn, the former US senator and co-founder of the Nuclear Threat Initiative, noted that Putin was engaged in 'nuclear folly' that significantly increased the prospect of a nuclear catastrophe.[3] In the same vein, former US State Department official Jeremy Shapiro

Jean-Yves Haine is a professor at the Sorbonne-Nouvelle Paris 3 and at Sciences Po. A shorter version of this article was published as a NATO Defense College Policy Brief in December 2022.

Survival | vol. 65 no. 1 | February–March 2023 | pp. 97–114   https://doi.org/10.1080/00396338.2023.2172856

reckoned that 'once an escalatory cycle begins, a series of individually rational steps can add up to a world-ending absurdity'.[4] Among scholars of strategic studies, John Mearsheimer argued that because Putin could not afford to lose in Ukraine, he would use 'every means available to avoid defeat', while George Perkovich saw the current situation as posing the greatest threat of nuclear use since 1962.[5] Carl Bildt, former prime minister of Sweden, declared that 'we are in a situation potentially more dangerous than the Cuban missile crisis'.[6]

How dangerous was the Cuban Missile Crisis? Is the analogy apt? What lessons can be drawn from the comparison?

How dangerous?

In a word, very. The US Strategic Air Command moved for the first time in its history to Defense Readiness Condition (DEFCON) 2, which among other measures called for readying 90 *Atlas* and 46 *Titan* intercontinental ballistic missiles for launch.[7] The Pentagon prepared an invasion force potentially comprising more than 100,000 troops for the biggest landing operation since the Second World War, and planned for thousands of airstrikes to destroy Cuban air defences.[8] When US president John F. Kennedy spoke on television on 22 October 1962, fear spread all over the world, triggering food-hoarding panics that stripped supermarkets bare. The public was calm only in Moscow, where the press did not mention the crisis until after the fact, characterising it as a 'squabble' involving nuclear missiles that took place in the Caribbean.[9]

Two factors significantly increased the risks of nuclear war during the 13-day stand-off between Moscow and Washington in October 1962: politics without strategy, and command without control.

The first factor turned on the way Kennedy framed the crisis. When presented with evidence of a nuclear-missile construction site in Cuba, his initial reaction was restrained. For him, this new element did not significantly affect the balance – or rather the imbalance – that existed between the Soviet Union and the United States. Washington enjoyed massive superiority in nuclear armaments, on the order of 17-to-1. Moreover, he acknowledged that the US had taken a comparable step by installing missiles in Turkey.[10]

Most of his senior military and policy advisers were not as sanguine. For them, the missiles in Cuba significantly reduced the US capacity to respond to an attack by shrinking the reaction time for a second strike and increasing the number of missiles that could hit the US. Moreover, they argued, US military superiority allowed for an easy military solution to this problem. They immediately pressured Kennedy to take the necessary steps for an invasion. Yet Kennedy and Robert S. McNamara, the secretary of defense, remained unmoved.

Although Kennedy did not initially consider the new situation in Cuba strategically critical, he came to understand that responding to it decisively, if not purely a matter of national security, was necessary for the US to maintain credibility, at home and abroad. US officials perceived the secrecy and deceit about the deployment of the missiles in Cuba as wilful Soviet provocation. Six weeks earlier, following the discovery of surface-to-air missiles in Cuba, Kennedy had publicly stated that the United States would not tolerate offensive weapons in Cuba, which would precipitate 'the gravest issues'.[11] Thus, the Soviets appeared to cross a red line.[12] Allies would have interpreted American acquiescence as a sign of weakness and hesitation. Any public compromise, including a possible quid pro quo between Soviet missiles in Cuba and US missiles in Turkey, could have implied that allied security was negotiable and threatened 'the end of NATO'.[13]

The main protagonists' spotty operational control also created serious risks. Kennedy ordered U-2 reconnaissance flights above Cuba to cease during the crisis, but some still took off. While Soviet leader Nikita Khrushchev had specifically asked Cuba not to operate Soviet SA-2 air-defence systems, the Cubans convinced deployed Soviet teams to activate them. On 27 October, a surface-to-air missile downed a U-2, killing the pilot.[14] On the same day, another U-2 taking radiation readings on Soviet nuclear tests over Siberia drifted into Soviet airspace, prompting six Soviet MiG fighters to give chase. A Joint Chiefs of Staff officer ordered the US Air Force to scramble F-102 interceptors to protect the U-2, unaware that they had been armed with nuclear missiles when the alert level was raised to DEFCON 2. A direct air-to-air confrontation was averted by a few minutes.[15] McNamara's order that US Navy ships drop only non-lethal depth charges to deter Soviet submarines spotted around the quarantine line established by Washington on 24 October was on occasion ignored.[16] American quarantine-enforcement operations could be ambiguous. In the Sargasso Sea, US destroyers dropped charges to force a Soviet submarine to the surface, where American planes circling 20 metres overhead and shining powerful searchlights fired cannon shells at short range as warning shots. The Soviet submarine commander, Valentin Savitsky, read this activity as the start of an actual attack, ordering an emergency dive and preparations for launching a nuclear-tipped torpedo. Such a launch required the assent of two more officers, and one, Captain Vasily Arkhipov, convinced the commander that the US ship was merely signalling rather than shooting to destroy.[17]

After tilting in favour of limited airstrikes against the missile sites in Cuba, the president, fearful of the possible consequences in Berlin, decided on a quarantine. Kennedy thus went from reluctant hawk to resolute dove. His choice of a quarantine rather than a more kinetic response afforded both sides time to open a dialogue and the ability to avoid misunderstandings through backchannels. Even so, nuclear strikes were avoided only by small margins. Ultimately, fear of unintended escalation was key to resolving the crisis. Will the same be said of the crisis over Ukraine?

A relevant analogy?

Analogies are tricky. On the one hand, an analogy may offer a short but simplified way to think about a complex reality by offering a template from which inferences are straightforward. On the other hand, the temptation to draw analogies poses risks of misrepresenting the past and misreading the present. The 'misuse' of history is common.[18] There are numerous material differences between the Cuban crisis and the Ukraine conflict, and any comparison must be a cautious exercise.

Firstly, the geopolitical landscape has significantly changed. The Cold War configuration in which two superpowers held strategic sway is gone. The international system is now multipolar, which makes the current conflict more complex and more global, but also potentially more tractable. The risks of horizontal escalation are higher, but so are the possibilities of restraint among allies and partners of an aggressor. China, which purportedly has a no-first-use nuclear doctrine, has clearly signalled to Moscow its refusal to support any use of nuclear weapons and its opposition to nuclear escalation, even if it is difficult to gauge the impact of Chinese pressure on Russia.[19] India too has indicated its opposition to Russian nuclear use. Global interconnectedness by trade and finance, and concomitant interdependence and vulnerability, can also have deterrent effects through sanctions and embargoes.[20]

Secondly, the normative environment is fundamentally different. Concerns about human rights have altered the understanding of sovereignty, increased accountability and diminished impunity. Globalisation has also reduced the benefit of conquest and the utility of force. Kantian ideals of perpetual peace and prosperity through trade became key elements of the European Union's identity and foreign policies. Yet what the EU regarded as inherently benevolent and beneficial, Russia perceived as unfriendly and hostile. Since Russia's seizure of Crimea in 2014, geopolitical dividing lines have thus resurfaced in Europe, to its considerable dismay.[21] The Russian invasion of Ukraine last February came as an enormous shock. At the same time, Moscow launched its invasion in the context of an international security regime through which the taboo against nuclear first use had been strengthened since the 1970s. Features of that regime include not only formal agreements such as the Nuclear Non-Proliferation Treaty, but also bilateral procedural safeguards and confidence-building mechanisms such as the nuclear hotline, now digital with instant translation, between senior US and Russian officials, which was a direct result of the Cuban Missile Crisis. Since that crisis, the theory of nuclear deterrence has also become far more refined, and deterrence itself presumptively more stable. The confrontation over the missiles in Cuba occurred in a far cruder and more tenuous international security environment.[22]

Thirdly, the crises themselves have very distinctive features. The Cuban Missile Crisis occurred in a very short time span – 13 days – while the current conflict in Ukraine has been going on for a year and counting, making the escalation rhythm much slower, even if very quick acceleration remains possible. The tight secrecy surrounding the crisis over Cuba bought Kennedy time to assemble a large team of experts and advisers before he elected to tell the world in his 22 October speech.[23] By contrast, the war in Ukraine has been quite public since it began. The Biden administration decided early to launch a proactive and public campaign of disclosures, including declassified intelligence, to test Putin's disposition and counter Russian disinformation. In addition, open-source information reinforced American messaging, further stripping away the once private nature of superpower conflict. All moves have been made public, strategic options announced, support operations revealed.[24]

Lastly, intelligence-gathering has fundamentally changed in terms of ubiquity, speed and accuracy. For purposes of guessing intentions and assessing capabilities, today's technologies are much more efficient, quick and precise than were U-2 overflights. In 1962, American decision-makers had no idea that nearly 100 tactical nuclear weapons were already stationed in Cuba, along with 42,000 Soviet troops. Contrary to the assessments of the US military, an American invasion of Cuba probably would have led to nuclear conflict.[25]

One prominent similarity between the two crises is mutual miscalculation. Kennedy did not comprehend the motives behind the Soviet Union's move – the defence of Cuba – because, at least after the Bay of Pigs debacle in 1961, he didn't consider the Caribbean island to be under threat. Khrushchev, for his part, completely failed to anticipate the United States' reaction to his gamble, blithely believing that it would accept the missiles as a fait accompli. Most European leaders didn't believe Russia would invade Ukraine, and Ukrainian President Volodymyr Zelenskyy himself, despite evidence presented by Washington, refused to publicly acknowledge the possibility until the last moment.[26] Putin, however, seriously underestimated the Ukrainians' military capabilities and NATO's willingness to support them. It remains extremely difficult to read Putin's intentions. If he continues to underrate Ukrainian resolve, he could become more tempted to use tactical nuclear weapons with an eye to ending the conflict quickly.

Russian nuclear risks, then and now

The two crises do share features that yield some useful parallels and a better understanding of the nuclear risks involved in Ukraine. The present crisis, like the earlier one, essentially involves a personalist dictator whose gamble has failed to deliver the expected results. Putin, like Khrushchev, is the ultimate decision-maker, and the supreme commander of the military, including nuclear forces. Although he does not have sole authority over nuclear use, it seems doubtful that someone in his sycophantic entourage would dare oppose his order.[27] He probably has not delegated authority to arm and launch nuclear weapons to battlefield commanders. Both Khrushchev and Kennedy cancelled such delegations of authority back in 1962. Russia, even after Putin's call on 27 February – three days after the invasion – to put deterrence forces 'on high combat alert', did not change its nuclear posture beyond routine systems checks, according to open sources. Russian tactical nuclear weapons have not been deployed on the battlefield, and any attempt to do so is likely to be spotted by Western intelligence.[28]

Putin may or may not share Khrushchev's fascination with rockets and nuclear power. Since the start of the crisis, though, he has repeated ad nauseam that Russia is the biggest nuclear power on earth, threatening on several occasions to use 'all necessary means' to 'defend' Russia and insisting that this was 'not a bluff'.[29] But his threats were mostly directed against the United States and NATO allies to keep them out of the conflict rather than towards Ukraine to gain territory, reinforcing mutual deterrence and diminishing the utility of nuclear coercion.

There is at least one salient reason that the Ukraine crisis may be more dangerous than the Cuban Missile Crisis. In 1962, Khrushchev blinked first because he did not consider Cuba an indispensable asset worthy of risking the end of the world. The deal that the United States offered – no US invasion and the withdrawal of medium-range *Jupiter* missiles from Turkey – was reasonable. With respect to Ukraine, the equities are roughly opposite. Since at least 2007, Putin has consistently asserted the crucial importance of Ukraine to Russia, which is central to his revanchist fury against NATO expansion. The Russian diplomatic service has echoed Putin's aggressive line and fed him reports tendentiously suggesting that his claims had met international approval.[30] This has fuelled Russia's broad escalation of the conflict, including the mobilisation of reservists, sham referendums in Russian-occupied territories and extensive missile strikes against Ukrainian infrastructure, as well as repeated threats to use nuclear weapons.[31]

Though the Russia–Ukraine war looks like a war of choice to most Western observers, Putin has effectively portrayed it as existential from his standpoint. But he may simply want his adversaries (and partners) to think that he looks at it that way. He still has the option of declaring victory, spouting some face-saving rhetoric and going home. Only if his incendiary rhetoric is fully credited as genuine is the conclusion that the war is existential for him justified, and there are reasons not to take his words at face value. Brinkmanship combined with backing down has been a hallmark of his approach in Ukraine so far. He may be using the 'existential war' characterisation to deter the West while contemplating Russia's exit. There is ample precedent for such behaviour. The Kremlin's anger and frustration evoke Richard Nixon's embrace of the 'madman theory' while trying to negotiate an end to the Vietnam War. Bluster, bombing and nuclear sabre-rattling didn't work then, and are unlikely to work now.[32]

At the same time, Putin's willingness to flirt with brinkmanship raises the question of his rationality. In the West, Putin has generally been considered a rational actor, one who cautiously calculates rather than recklessly gambles. Since the start of the war, however, his errors on the battlefield have been many, casting doubt on his capacity for intelligent decision-making and, possibly, assessing the Western appetite for military escalation. Some experts have underlined his isolation, others his paranoia; most still believe he is not suicidal.[33] Yet concerns about his leadership status and obsession with avoiding failure may have increased his propensity for wishful thinking and inclination to invite bolstering analyses, and thus distorted his decisions. In this connection, too, it is instructive to recall the Cuban Missile Crisis.

In the early 1960s, Khrushchev desperately sought to have Moscow treated as an equal by Washington, which in his mind required strategic parity. Cuba offered him a shortcut. Overconfident and inattentive to unwelcome information, Khrushchev's decision to send missiles to Cuba displayed 'strong evidence' of bolstering.[34] Likewise, Putin seems consumed with securing great-power status and international standing. Clearly he seeks Russia's restoration as a great power, and perceives the West as dominant and hostile. Beyond that, he harbours an ironclad determination to avenge the fall of the Soviet Empire, thereby securing a privileged place for himself in the Russian pantheon.[35] Putin's belief in Russia's singular destiny led him to gamble in Ukraine. It has not paid off. To avoid being seen as weak or incompetent, and indeed to evade military defeat, Putin may double down on the gamble, with potentially devastating consequences. Then again, he could also redefine success, declare victory and walk away.

Putin's desperation to appear victorious could affect his rational cost–benefit calculation regarding the use of tactical nuclear weapons. Strategically, these weapons have no chance of succeeding, whether used to demonstrate resolve, gain territory or compel Ukraine's submission.[36] In Ukraine as in Cuba, the main worry is that political considerations – domestic survival and international reputation – may trump strategy. In this vein, one key constraint would be that two important partners – China and India – would be deeply disenchanted by Russia's use of nuclear weapons, which cuts against unleashing them to preserve Russia's reputation, especially when Russia's allies are so few.

Lessons for NATO
As to how NATO should respond, the Cuban Missile Crisis offers noteworthy parallels. The first relates to the perception and management of risks. In 1962, Kennedy chose to minimise the risks of direct conflict, rejecting a conventional invasion of Cuba, because it would have led to a Soviet response in West Berlin, which in turn would have left him with 'only one alternative, which is to fire nuclear weapons, which is a hell of an alternative'.[37] Yet inaction was equally impossible. Thus, a middle ground was chosen and a carefully calibrated course of action was preferred.[38] Kennedy understood that the quarantine could go very wrong, but assessed that it was the least risky alternative short of doing nothing.

Kennedy was very pessimistic about deterrence and thus extremely careful.[39] Biden seems more bullish on its viability and thus more assertive. Putin's nuclear threats have served to limit the potential for direct Western intervention in the conflict, and have slowed (but not stopped) the West's provision of higher-end weapons systems. Military assistance to Ukraine was initially restricted to defensive systems. Some weapons – including American surface-to-surface missiles with ranges exceeding 300 km and

Polish MiG-29 fighters – were therefore excluded. In January, however, the United Kingdom decided to send *Challenger* 2 tanks to Ukraine.[40] Germany has declined to supply *Leopard* tanks not because they are afraid of crossing a line, but because the tanks will not be war-ready before 2024.[41]

On balance, Putin's attempt to increase the scale of nuclear coercion has been a failure. Observing and implicitly insisting on the evolved and accepted terms of deterrence, the West has crossed multiple Russian red lines to date without consequence.[42] When Putin's nuclear threats became too widely coercive and applied to outcomes outside his core interests, and his false-flag operations – as with the dirty-bomb plot – too obvious, Biden firmly warned him of potentially 'catastrophic consequences' if a tactical nuclear device were detonated in Ukraine. The possibility of 'escalate to de-escalate' tactics involving nuclear weapons might seem to intensify as the Russian army suffers setbacks, but the prospect of losing allied support would discourage them.[43] Reinforcing the point, the White House has reminded the Kremlin that the use of even a low-yield nuclear weapon would trigger a compelling American response.

The Biden administration is travelling a judicious path on which neither those who want justice nor those who want peace are liable to be satisfied.[44] For NATO, this course increases the risks of division, and it is made riskier by potential errors, loss of control and accidents – all crucial factors during the Cuban Missile Crisis. In Ukraine, NATO is not in direct confrontation with Russia, so escalation takes place in slow motion. Yet, since February 2022, several incidents could easily have led to disastrous, unintended consequences. Ukraine has 15 nuclear power plants, some of which have been targeted. Explosions at the Pivdennoukrainsk plant, near Mykolaiv, were a mere 300 metres from the reactor, and constant shelling has left the power plant in Zaporizhzhia without a safe source of backup power, leading Rafael Grossi, director of the International Atomic Energy Agency, to describe it as 'an unsustainable and increasingly precarious situation'.[45] Likewise, there have been several tense encounters between NATO countries and Russia. In September 2022, a Russian submarine was spotted in French territorial waters and duly escorted out.[46] Later in September, one of two Russian Su-27 fighter aircraft that were shadowing a Royal Air Force surveillance plane over the Black Sea – not unusual by itself – fired a missile.[17] On 15 November 2022, a rocket hit Przewodów, Poland, killing two Polish citizens and causing considerable strategic anxiety until it was determined that it was an errant strike originating in Ukraine. Major incidents have been avoided but seem likely to arise.

NATO must also manage Ukrainian concerns and expectations. In 1962, the only player enthusiastic about using nuclear weapons was Cuban leader Fidel Castro. When he asked Khrushchev to use all necessary means to defend Cuba, including pre-emptive nuclear strikes on Washington, the Soviet premier thought Castro had gone insane.[48] With respect to Ukraine, the terms are different but the logic is the same. If the war turns increasingly in Russia's favour, Zelenskyy's calls for more aid will increase, possibly including direct intervention.[49] If Ukraine forces a Russian withdrawal, fighting for every square kilometre of occupied Ukrainian territory, including Crimea, may provoke Putin. It would be vexing to restrain a deservedly triumphant Ukraine or to reward a deservedly vanquished Russia, but, under the nuclear shadow, moderation would have to remain a NATO imperative.

*   *   *

Perhaps the paramount lesson from Cuba is the necessity of dialogue. In October 1962, Kennedy was adamant about the need to maintain official diplomatic communications and backchannels with Moscow. Today, both Russia and the US have kept communication lines open.[50] Dialogue remains necessary to signal resolve and thus strengthen deterrence, and to clarify intentions and thus avoid miscalculation. To escape nuclear brinkmanship, bilateral talks between the US and Russia should continue while Ukraine considers at what point peace talks will need to begin, especially given that, with a second year of warfare approaching, prospects of territorial gains are still tantalising for both sides. Peace without total victory may be preferable to victory in total ruin. But the conclusion of the war is likely to turn on Putin finding a way to save face rather than Ukraine giving up large swathes of occupied territory.

Notes

1 Quoted in David E. Sanger, 'Biden
Turns to Lessons from the Cuban
Missile Crisis to Deal with Putin's
Nuclear Threat', *New York Times*, 29
October 2022, https://www.nytimes.
com/2022/10/09/world/europe/
biden-turns-to-lessons-from-the-
cuban-missile-crisis-to-deal-with-
putins-nuclear-threat.html.

2 Quoted in Brendan Cole, 'Putin May
Hit Back with Nuclear Weapons Amid
Ukraine Counter: Ex-NATO Chief',
Newsweek, 13 September 2022, https://
www.newsweek.com/russia-ukraine-
nato-nuclear-gottemoeller-1742533.

3 Quoted in Eric Schlosser, 'What If
Russia Uses Nuclear Weapons in
Ukraine?', *Atlantic*, 20 June 2022,
https://www.theatlantic.com/ideas/
archive/2022/06/russia-ukraine-
nuclear-weapon-us-response/661315/.

4 Jeremy Shapiro, 'We Are On a
Path to Nuclear War', *War on the
Rocks*, 12 October 2022, https://
warontherocks.com/2022/10/
the-end-of-the-world-is-nigh/.

5 John J. Mearsheimer, 'Playing With Fire
in Ukraine: The Underappreciated Risks
of Catastrophic Escalation', *Foreign
Affairs*, 17 August 2022, https://www.
foreignaffairs.com/ukraine/playing-
fire-ukraine. Perkovich quoted in '60
ans après la crise de Cuba, l'idée d'une
guerre nucléaire de nouveau plausible',
La Croix, 20 October 2022, https://
www.la-croix.com/60-ans-crise-Cuba-
idee-guerre-nucleaire-nouveau-plausi
ble-2022-10-20-1301238555.

6 Carl Bildt, 'This Is Best Way to
Counter Putin's Nuclear Threats',
Washington Post, 10 October 2022,
https://www.washingtonpost.com/
opinions/2022/10/10/putin-russia-
nuclear-threat-deterrence/.

7 See Scott D. Sagan, 'Nuclear Alerts
and Crisis Management', *International
Security*, vol. 9, no. 4, Spring 1985, pp.
99–139. The shift to DEFCON 2 was
supposed to be transmitted secretly,
but it was not, and the Soviets took
notice. See Raymond L. Garthoff,
*Reflections on the Cuban Missile
Crisis* (Washington DC: Brookings
Institution, 1989), p. 62.

8 See Michael C. Desch, '"That Deep
Mud in Cuba": The Strategic Threat
and U.S. Planning for a Conventional
Response During the Missile Crisis',
Security Studies, vol. 1, no. 2, Winter
1991, pp. 317–51.

9 See Spencer R. Weart, *Nuclear Fear:
A History of Images* (Cambridge, MA:
Harvard University Press, 1988), p. 259.

10 Khrushchev often said to visitors to his
home along the Black Sea, 'Can't you
see? US missiles in Turkey, aimed at
my dacha!' Quoted in Philip Nash, *The
Other Missiles of October: Eisenhower,
Kennedy and the Jupiters, 1957–1963*
(Chapel Hill, NC: University of North
Carolina Press, 1997), p. 106.

11 US Department of State, 'Statement by
President John F. Kennedy on Cuba,
September 4, 1962', *Bulletin*, vol. 47,
no. 1,213, 24 September 1962, p. 450.
Kennedy explicitly rejected the option
of a blockade because it would have
triggered the same response by the
Soviets against Berlin.

12 Kennedy recognised the dilemma,
noting that 'last month, I said we
weren't going to allow it. Last month,

I should have said that we don't care. But when we said we're not going to, and then they go and do it, and then we do nothing, I would think that our risks increase … After all, this is a political struggle as much as military.' Quoted in Ernest R. May and Philip D. Zelikow (eds), *The Kennedy Tapes: Inside the White House During the Cuban Missile Crisis* (Cambridge, MA: Belknap Press, 1997), p. 92. Theodore Sorensen, White House counsel at the time and Kennedy's confidant, later commented: 'I believe the President drew the line precisely where he thought the Soviets were not and would not be.' Quoted in James G. Blight and David A. Welch, *On the Brink: Americans and Soviets Reexamine the Cuban Missile Crisis* (New York: Hill and Wang, 1989), p. 43.

13 The missiles in Turkey were of course withdrawn, but the deal remained secret for 30 years. McGeorge Bundy, Kennedy's national security advisor, summed up the conundrum: 'If we appear to be trading the defense of Turkey for a threat to Cuba, we'll just have to face a radical decline in the effectiveness of the NATO alliance.' Quoted in Jean-Yves Haine, 'Kennedy, Kroutchev et les missiles de Cuba: Choix rationnel et responsabilité individuelle', *Cultures et Conflits*, no. 36, Winter 1999–Spring 2000, p. 136.

14 See James G. Blight, Bruce J. Allyn and David A. Welch, *Cuba on the Brink: Castro, the Missile Crisis and the Soviet Collapse* (New York: Pantheon, 1993), p. 113.

15 See Dave Kindy, 'Forgotten U-2 Pilots Helped End the Cuban Missile Crisis 60 Years Ago', *Washington Post,* 23 October 2022, https://www.washingtonpost.com/history/2022/10/23/cuban-missile-crisis-u2-pilots/.

16 Some sailors, frustrated to be required to use blanks, stuffed grenades into these charges, and when they exploded near a sub's hull, the noise was like 'being inside an oil drum beaten by a sledgehammer'. See Julian Borger, 'Cuban Missile Crisis, 60 Years On: New Papers Reveal How Close the World Came to Nuclear Disaster', *Guardian*, 27 October 2022, https://www.theguardian.com/world/2022/oct/27/cuban-missile-crisis-60-years-on-new-papers-reveal-how-close-the-world-came-to-nuclear-disaster.

17 Lyndon Johnson, the vice president, had warned McNamara about the routine: 'If you are going to try to psychologically scare them with flares, you are liable to get your bottom shot at.' Serhii Plokhy, *Nuclear Folly*: *A New History of the Cuban Missile Crisis* (New York: Penguin, 2021), p. 271. See also Svetlana Savranskaya, 'New Sources on the Role of Soviet Submarines in the Cuban Missile Crisis', *Journal of Strategic Studies*, vol. 28, no. 2, April 2005, pp. 233–59.

18 See Ernest R. May, *The Lessons of the Past: The Use and Misuse of History in American Foreign Policy* (Oxford: Oxford University Press, 1973), the seminal book on this topic. See also Yuen Foong Khong, *Analogies at War: Korea, Munich, Dien Bien Phu, and the Vietnam Decisions of 1965* (Princeton, NJ: Princeton University Press, 1992).

19 In December 2013, a joint declaration by Beijing and Kyiv stipulated that China would not use or threaten to

use nuclear weapons against Ukraine and, more importantly, that China would provide Ukraine with security assurances in the event of any such threat by a third party. Zhou Bo, 'China Can Use Its Leverage with Russia to Prevent a Nuclear War', *Financial Times*, 27 October 2022, https://www.ft.com/content/fo5fef3f-a8be-4007-a161-34764419847f.

[20] Ten years ago, one-quarter of Ukraine's exports went to Russia, and roughly the same proportion to Europe. In 2019, only 8% of Ukraine's exports went to Russia, while the EU's share shot up to 42.6%. Georg Zachmann, Marek Dabrowski and Marta Domínguez-Jiménez, 'Ukraine: Trade Reorientation from Russia to the EU', Bruegel, 13 July 2020, https://www.bruegel.org/blog-post/ukraine-trade-reorientation-russia-eu. Ukraine's economic integration with Europe infuriated Putin.

[21] See Richard Sakwa, 'The Death of Europe? Continental Fates After Ukraine', *International Affairs*, vol. 91, no. 3, May 2015, pp. 553–79.

[22] During the Trump administration, the nuclear taboo arguably weakened, but it still appears to be stronger than it was in 1962. See Seyom Brown, 'The New Nuclear MADness', *Survival*, vol. 62, no. 1, February–March 2020, pp. 63–88; and Nina Tannenwald, 'How Strong Is the Nuclear Taboo Today?', *Washington Quarterly*, vol. 41, no. 3, Fall 2018, pp. 89–109.

[23] All it took was one phone call to James Reston, then the *New York Times*'s Washington bureau chief, to silence journalists. See, for example, Max Frankel, *High Noon in the Cold War:*

Kennedy, Khrushchev and the Cuban Missile Crisis (New York: Ballantine, 2004). The pressure on the Kennedy administration to invade Cuba would have been far greater in today's high-tempo media environment and 24-hour news cycle.

[24] See Joshua Yaffa and Adam Entous, 'Inside the High-Stakes Fight to Control the Narrative on Ukraine', *New Yorker*, 21 February 2022.

[25] See Raymond L. Garthoff, 'New Evidence on the Cuban Missile Crisis: Khrushchev, Nuclear Weapons, and the Cuban Missile Crisis', *Cold War International History Project Bulletin*, no. 11, Winter 1998, pp. 251–62.

[26] See Shane Harris et al., 'Road to War: US Struggled to Convince Allies, and Zelensky, of Risk of Invasion', *Washington Post*, 16 August 2022, https://www.washingtonpost.com/national-security/interactive/2022/ukraine-road-to-war/.

[27] Authority over the use of nuclear weapons appears to lie with three Russian officials: the president, the defence minister and the chief of the general staff. It seems that at least two out of the three must assent for an order to launch nuclear weapons to be issued. Defence Minister Sergei Shoigu's and Chief of the General Staff Valery Gerasimov's views on the use of tactical nuclear weapons remain unknown. See Kristin Ven Bruusgaard, 'Understanding Putin's Nuclear Decision-making', *War on the Rocks*, 22 March 2022, https://warontherocks.com/2022/03/understanding-putins-nuclear-decision-making/.

[28] See Eric Schlosser, 'What If Russia Uses Nuclear Weapons in Ukraine?',

Atlantic, 20 June 2022, https://www.theatlantic.com/ideas/archive/2022/06/russia-ukraine-nuclear-weapon-us-response/661315/.

29 Joseph Cirincione, 'Putin Says Nuclear Threat Is No Bluff. We Should Take Him at His Word', *Washington Post*, 26 September 2022, https://www.washingtonpost.com/opinions/2022/09/26/putin-nuclear-threat-bluff-us-biden-response/. Because the threat to use nuclear weapons may seem outlandish, reputation is an important tool to make such a threat appear credible. 'This tension leads to the following paradox: nuclear weapons cause actors to worry more about their own reputation than before, even though it seems that policymakers would be less likely than before to use others' reputation as a guide to behavior in a crisis.' Jonathan Mercer, *Reputation and International Politics* (Ithaca, NY: Cornell University Press, 1996), p. 222.

30 Quoted in David Ignatius, 'Putin Warned the West 15 Years Ago. Now, in Ukraine, He's Poised to Wage War', *Washington Post*, 20 February 2022, https://www.washingtonpost.com/opinions/2022/02/20/putin-ukraine-nato-2007-munich-conference/.

31 Ten days before the invasion of Ukraine, Finnish President Sauli Niinistö, who knows Putin well, acknowledged: 'I don't know what Putin thinks. But Russia is willing to pay high prices for what it considers to be important.' Quoted in an interview conducted by Christian Esch and Christoph Scheuermann, '"Suddenly, He Started to Behave in a Very, Very Decisive Way"', *Spiegel International*, 14 February 2022, https://www.spiegel.de/international/world/finnish-president-sauli-niinistoe-on-putin-and-the-ukraine-conflict-a-bb9281d3-2cc6-49a1-87eb-199569991c79.

32 See, for example, Robert Jervis et al., 'Nuclear Weapons, Coercive Diplomacy, and the Vietnam War: Perspectives on Nixon's Nuclear Spector', *Journal of Cold War Studies*, vol. 19, no. 4, Fall 2017, pp. 192–210; and Gideon Rose, 'What Nixon's Endgame Reveals About Putin's', *Foreign Affairs*, 14 October 2022, https://www.foreignaffairs.com/ukraine/what-nixons-endgame-reveals-about-putins.

33 As a former Russian diplomat noted, 'the war is a stark demonstration of how decisions made in echo chambers can backfire'. Boris Bondarev, 'The Sources of Russian Misconduct', *Foreign Affairs*, vol. 101, no. 6, November/December 2022, p. 39. See also Michael McFaul, 'The West Shouldn't Back Down in the Face of Putin's Threats', *Washington Post*, 13 April 2022, https://www.washingtonpost.com/opinions/2022/04/13/west-help-ukraine-win-next-phase-russia/.

34 In both foreign and domestic affairs, Khrushchev behaved like 'a roulette player'. Fyodor Burlatsky and Georgy Shakhnazarov, who had been aides to Khrushchev, called him *azartnyi*, which means, 'reckless' or 'hot-headed'. Quoted in May and Zelikow, *The Kennedy Tapes*, pp. 668–9. In September 1962, after US surveillance planes detected Soviet surface-to-air missiles in Cuba and Kennedy publicly indicated that the

deployment of offensive Soviet missiles would raise 'the gravest issues', Khrushchev actually accelerated the transport of nuclear weapons to Cuba. See Aleksandr Fursenko and Timothy Naftali, 'The Pitsunda Decision: Khrushchev and Nuclear Weapons', Cold War International History Project, Bulletin 10, March 1998, pp. 223–7, https://www.wilsoncenter.org/sites/default/files/media/documents/publication/CWIHPBulletin10_p6.pdf; and Plokhy, *Nuclear Folly*. On bolstering, see Richard Ned Lebow and Janice Gross Stein, *We All Lost the Cold War* (Princeton, NJ: Princeton University Press, 1997), p. 88.

35 'Rumour has it that, asked who are Vladimir Putin's most trusted advisers, one of his inner circle members replied drily: "Ivan the Terrible, Catherine the Great and Peter the Great."' Quoted in Ivan Krastev, 'Putin's Aggressive Autocracy Reduces Russian Soft Power to Ashes', *Financial Times*, 16 June 2022, https://www.ft.com/content/f9bcb5ac-ab05-4630-b641-ca3db-dbe4666. See also David Remnick, 'What Is Putin Thinking?', *New Yorker*, 27 March 2022; and Fiona Hill and Angela Stent, 'The World Putin Wants', *Foreign Affairs*, vol. 101, no. 5, September/October 2022, pp. 108–22.

36 See William Alberque, 'Russia Is Unlikely to Use Nuclear Weapons in Ukraine', IISS Analysis, 10 October 2022, https://www.iiss.org/blogs/analysis/2022/10/russia-is-unlikely-to-use-nuclear-weapons-in-ukraine; Isaac Chotiner, 'How Close Is Vladimir Putin to Using a Nuclear Bomb?', *New Yorker*, 11 October 2022, https://

www.newyorker.com/news/q-and-a/how-close-is-vladimir-putin-to-using-a-nuclear-bomb; and J. Andrés Gannon, 'If Russia Goes Nuclear: Three Scenarios for the Ukraine War', Council on Foreign Relations, 9 November 2022, https://www.cfr.org/article/if-russia-goes-nuclear-three-scenarios-ukraine-war.

37 On Berlin, see Thomas Risse-Kappen, *Cooperation Among Democracies: The European Influence on US Foreign Policy* (Princeton, NJ: Princeton University Press, 1995), pp. 160–1. The US Joint Chiefs of Staff, however, believed that the Soviets would refrain from seizing West Berlin because the US had an overwhelming strategic advantage, and because the Soviets were, as General Curtis LeMay put it, 'rational people'. See Richard Rhodes, 'The General and World War III', *New Yorker*, 19 June 1995, pp. 47–59.

38 McNamara said that 'all of the routes [to get the missiles out of Cuba] could lead into disaster … We should not accept even a small risk in any of them.' Quoted in Blight and Welch, *On the Brink*, p. 188.

39 This follows an observation made by Albert Wohlstetter, noted in Pierre Hassner, 'Au delà de l'abstraction stratégique', *Commentaire*, vol. 32, no. 4, 1985, p. 1,019.

40 See Jonathan Beale and Jasmine Andersson, 'UK to Send Challenger 2 Tanks to Ukraine, Rishi Sunak Confirms', BBC News, 14 January 2023, https://www.bbc.co.uk/news/uk-64274755.

41 See Charlie Cooper, 'German Arms Firm Rheinmetall Says Leopard

Tanks Can't Be Ready for Ukraine Until 2024', *Politico*, 15 January 2022, https://www.politico.eu/article/ukraine-war-germany-tanks-rheinmetall-leopard-2024/.

42 See Jonathan Stevenson and Steven Simon, 'Why Putin Went Straight for the Nuclear Threat', *New York Times*, 1 April 2022, https://www.nytimes.com/2022/04/01/opinion/biden-putin-ukraine-nuclear-weapons.html.

43 On the subtleties of the 'escalate to de-escalate' concept in Russian nuclear policy, see Dave Johnson, 'Russia's Deceptive Nuclear Policy', *Survival*, vol. 63, no. 3, June–July 2021, pp. 123–42.

44 Raymond Aron said it six decades ago: 'The call of wisdom is always contested, it will not satisfy the moralists or the Machiavelli followers.' Raymond Aron, *Paix et Guerres entre les Nations* (Paris: Calmann-Lévy, 1962), p. 596. On potential divisions among allies, see Ivan Krastev and Mark Leonard, 'Peace Versus Justice: The Coming European Split Over the War in Ukraine', Policy Brief, European Council on Foreign Relations, 15 June 2022, https://ecfr.eu/publication/peace-versus-justice-the-coming-european-split-over-the-war-in-ukraine/.

45 See Charles Casto, 'How to Prevent a Crisis at the Zaporizhia Nuclear Power Plant', *The Economist*, 6 September 2022, https://www.economist.com/by-invitation/2022/09/06/how-to-prevent-a-crisis-at-the-zaporizhia-nuclear-power-plant-according-to-a-fukushima-veteran.

46 Since then, France has had three of its four nuclear-armed submarines on continuous sea patrol, an unprecedented situation.

47 Russia said it was 'a technical malfunction'. Intercepted communications indicated that it resulted from a decision of the pilot rather than an order from Moscow. As UK Defence Secretary Ben Wallace said, 'We do not consider it a deliberate escalation … We are incredibly lucky that it did not become worse.' Quoted in John Paul Rathbone, 'Russian Jet "Released" Missile Near UK Spy Plane over Black Sea', *Financial Times*, 20 October 2022, https://www.ft.com/content/0d707a99-af54-475e-b725-71547a4d0f2d.

48 Fortunately, Castro had no control over the tactical nuclear weapons already on the island, as Khrushchev had revoked the delegation of authority that would have allowed Cuban soldiers to operate them on 22 October. See Aleksandr Fursenko and Timothy Naftali, *Khrushchev's Cold War: The Inside Story of an American Adversary* (New York: W. W. Norton & Company, 2006), p. 473. On Castro's missive to Khrushchev, see James Hershberg, 'Fidel Castro, Nuclear War and the Missile Crisis: Three Missing Soviet Cables', *Cold War International History Project Bulletin*, no. 17/18, Fall 2012, pp. 327–9.

49 On 6 October 2022, Zelenskyy, when asked about NATO's role in the conflict, called for the international community to 'do preemptive strikes' instead of 'waiting for Russian nuclear strikes'. 'A Special Address by Volodymyr Zelenskyy, President of Ukraine', Lowy Institute, 6 October 2022, https://www.lowyinstitute.org/event/special-address-volodymyr-zelenskyy-president-ukraine.

50 US National Security Advisor Jake Sullivan has confirmed that

communication channels between Washington and Moscow remain open. Vivian Salama and Michael R. Gordon, 'Senior White House Official Involved in Undisclosed Talks with Top Putin Aides', *Wall Street Journal*, 7 November 2022, https://www.wsj.com/articles/senior-white-house-official-involved-in-undisclosed-talks-with-top-putin-aides-11667768988.

The Resilience Requirement: Responding to China's Rise as a Technology Power

Andrew B. Kennedy

China's rise as a technology power in recent years is striking. In areas ranging from quantum communications to 5G networks to hypersonic weaponry, China is making a mark on the global technological landscape. The country is constrained by many challenges, including a stifling political environment, sluggish state enterprises and an underdeveloped financial system – not to mention a daunting international environment. Despite these and other problems, however, China's growing technological capabilities have become impossible to ignore.[1]

This presents the United States and its partners with a difficult dilemma. They can remain open to collaborating with China in pursuit of several benefits: scientific knowledge, economic prosperity and China's constructive dependence on the outside world. Yet openness risks fuelling China's rise in worrisome ways, especially since foreign technologies and know-how may be channelled into the Chinese military or into Orwellian-sounding internal-surveillance and -monitoring systems that tighten the government's political control. Reducing openness mitigates these risks, but it also limits the rewards while intensifying China's pursuit of technological self-reliance and potentially exacerbating differences between Washington and its partners.

Andrew B. Kennedy is an associate professor at Crawford School of Public Policy at the Australian National University. The research for this article was supported by the Australian Department of Defence under Grant 2020-106-083. The views expressed herein are those of the author and are not necessarily those of the Australian government or the Australian Department of Defence.

Survival | vol. 65 no. 1 | February–March 2023 | pp. 115–128   https://doi.org/10.1080/00396338.2023.2172858

In recent years, the United States has shifted towards reducing openness. During the Trump administration, American measures included higher tariffs on China's high-tech exports, tighter investment screening and targeted restrictions on key companies such as Huawei. While the Biden administration's approach is evolving, the trend towards restraining technological interaction has deepened in important respects. Most notably, the Biden administration unveiled new restrictions in late 2022 to limit China's ability to access advanced computing chips, develop and maintain supercomputers, and manufacture sophisticated semiconductors. The restrictions appear carefully crafted to have an impact without giving key firms sufficient incentive to 'de-Americanise' their supply chains.[2] Nevertheless, additional restrictions are expected, and some version of high-tech 'decoupling' between the United States and China is clearly in progress, though it remains unclear how far it will go.[3]

Decoupling is undoubtedly warranted in some cases, particularly in areas where the risks of openness are acute and the rewards seem limited. Yet it is also important to appreciate the downsides of decoupling, some of which are already apparent. The Chinese government has intensified its push for increased technological self-reliance, and the multiplying restrictions have given Chinese firms a greater incentive to cooperate with it, which is likely to yield more technological progress than in the past.[4] To the extent that this push succeeds, there will be fewer opportunities for foreign firms in China, and reduced leverage for the developed countries on which China has relied in the past. It is also unclear how far US allies and partners will travel down the decoupling road, and some are clearly concerned about the prospect of a 'new Cold War'.[5] Many forms of interaction between China and the outside world will undoubtedly continue.

While decoupling is a critical tool for the United States and its partners, it should not be the only one, and may not be the most important. They must also develop greater resilience – that is, the ability to bounce back after an adverse shock, either by absorbing it or by changing practices in response to it.[6] Resilience provides essential context for risk-and-reward calculations: resilient actors can afford to take some risks in pursuit of rewards, while those lacking resilience are more constrained.

There are many ways to promote greater resilience in this case, including new measures to defend against cyber-enabled espionage and new high-tech initiatives among partners. While some work on these fronts is under way, it remains grossly inadequate given the scale of the challenge. As a result, collective efforts to strengthen resilience continue to be overshadowed by the drive for decoupling. Going forward, strengthening resilience should become a much higher priority for the United States and its partners than it has been to date.

A vexing challenge

Coping with China's rise as a technology power has never been easy. Since the 1980s, globalisation and economic reform in China have created vast new opportunities for commerce and collaboration with the outside world, even as the number of high-tech products with both civilian and military applications has multiplied. As a result, policymakers in many developed countries have had to balance their strategic interests against the economic opportunities presented by China's development.[7] In recent years, striking this balance has become more difficult, since both the risks and the rewards of openness are growing.

The risks are increasing for several reasons. For one, it has become more difficult to ensure that collaboration with civilian entities in China will not accelerate the Chinese military's modernisation. Since the mid-2010s, China has stepped up its pursuit of 'military–civil fusion', an initiative that seeks to integrate civilian and defence technologies and production systems. While there are many obstacles to military–civil fusion in China, President Xi Jinping has personally led the integration effort, and it appears to have made headway. In 2018, a People's Liberation Army acquisitions expert disclosed that 1,800 civilian entities had acquired equipment-contractor certificates, which allow them to work with the military in areas ranging from scientific research to tech-support services, while 1,189 civilian entities had acquired weapons and equipment-research and -production licences, which permit them to work on weapons systems. Roughly 50 of the latter have apparently acquired the most sensitive type of licence and are believed to be working in specialised areas such as uninhabited systems, nanotechnology and microminiature-scale technologies. The drive for military–civil fusion is believed to have enlisted participation from some of China's leading civilian firms, including Huawei, Alibaba and DJI, which manufactures drones.[8]

Collaboration with civilian entities in China may also involve actors engaged in other activities that arouse concern. Chinese intelligence agencies have apparently enlisted leading technology firms to identify useful pieces of information in the reams of data acquired through espionage.[9] Since 2017, in fact, tech companies have been required by law to cooperate with intelligence agencies. And while some Chinese artificial-intelligence (AI) firms have been censured abroad for supporting Beijing's efforts to track ethnic minorities, particularly in Xinjiang, the Chinese government's ambitions go well beyond controlling such groups. Beijing aspires to develop a system to monitor China's entire population, prompting comparisons to Michel Foucault's 'panopticon', and it has intensified efforts to influence media reporting and opinion overseas.[10] While these efforts are fraught with challenges, the point is that private Chinese firms play important roles in them. In pursuit of profit, in fact, some private firms have created monitoring applications that go well beyond what government officials originally envisioned.[11]

China is also increasingly capable of pilfering foreign technology and data for economic purposes through cyber espionage and other means. The United States and China agreed not to conduct or support cyber-enabled theft of intellectual property in 2015, and that agreement seemed to have a positive effect for a while. In recent years, however, economically motivated cyber espionage emanating from China has revived, led by the Ministry of State Security. Its cyber operations appear relatively sophisticated, and the ministry also employs contractors to augment its capacity and tradecraft. There is also evidence that the ministry coordinates its efforts in cyberspace with human-intelligence operations to maximise impact.[12] In the future, it is expected that emerging technologies including 5G, AI and quantum computing will make it easier for China's cyber spies to capture, transfer, decrypt and process data.[13]

Lastly, there are the dangers posed by technological dependence on China. Other major powers have long known the general risks of dependence on the large and growing Chinese market, given the leverage such dependence could potentially offer Beijing.[14] The risk of depending on China for new technologies has arisen more recently. China plays, or seeks to play, a leading role in a growing number of high-tech supply chains, including high-speed rail, 5G communications and AI. Its technological leadership has the potential to increase China's influence over countries that depend on these supply chains. It could also afford Beijing opportunities to shape emerging technologies in line with its own values and priorities. It is against this backdrop that concerns about technological dependence on China have recently become evident in some European countries.[15]

Despite the real and increasing risks, the outside world cannot simply turn its back on China. The rewards of interaction are too great, and they are likely to increase over time in important respects. While the US government has become more wary of students from China, for example, these students are a valuable source of brainpower for the United States. In fact, China sends more students abroad than any other country. As of 2021–22, more than 290,000 Chinese students were enrolled at US universities – 31% of all foreign students there – and roughly 123,000 were graduate students. Foreign students also enrich the labour pool in their host countries following graduation. In 2021, 74% of Chinese students receiving doctoral degrees from US universities intended to remain in the United States.[16] As the COVID-19 pandemic recedes, Chinese student flows could increase significantly.

The outside world cannot turn its back on China

China has also become far and away the leading source of foreign collaboration for US scientists, and a key partner for other developed countries as well.[17] There is strong evidence that Chinese scientists contribute a great deal to these collaborations.[18] Between 2012 and 2021, China's score in the Nature Index, which tracks the affiliations of researchers publishing in the world's most highly regarded scientific journals, jumped from 24% to 84% of the US score.[19] China's contributions will undoubtedly grow as its investment in basic research does. In 2021, that investment rose 24% to 182 billion yuan. That was 6.5% of China's total research and development (R&D) spending, and the government's goal is to increase that figure to 8% by 2025.[20]

China's scientific collaboration with developed countries – particularly the United States – has waned in recent years, but this is partly due to the COVID pandemic, and there is still great potential. Joint work on green technology should be a particular priority, considering the urgency of addressing climate change and China's importance in this effort. The US–China Clean Energy Research Center was established in 2011, and it quickly became active and productive. Making such enterprises multilateral would help insulate them from the turbulence of US–China relations. Other research areas hold promise as well, particularly those that are less politically sensitive.[21] Even in sensitive areas like cyber security, academic collaboration focused on defensive measures could prove mutually beneficial.[22]

Multinational firms may reap rewards from conducting R&D in China. R&D centres in countries such as China and India allow foreign multinationals to tap into local expertise that complements that available in their home countries. Combining the expertise of multiple countries – each with differing strengths – could surmount what appear to be diminishing returns to purely domestic innovation efforts in developed countries.[23] Drawing on Chinese expertise may become increasingly attractive as its distinctive strengths continue to advance. China has by far the world's largest market for electric vehicles, for example, and it is poised to lead this industry. Tesla has invested in a comprehensive R&D facility in Shanghai, which is expected to rival its US counterpart in scale.[24] More broadly, foreign firms often conduct R&D in China to adapt their products to local requirements and preferences, better enabling them to compete in that market. While doing business in China has become more difficult, many multinationals – including tech firms – remain committed to competing for Chinese customers.[25]

Given the risks and rewards of openness, it is clearly inadvisable for foreign governments to focus only on one or the other. Some kind of balance must be struck. In any case, they will also need to become more resilient.

The search for resilience

The concept of resilience has been applied across a wide range of domains, including psychology, sociology and engineering, as well as the study of international politics.[26] Resilience may manifest in the ability of individuals, organisations or nations to absorb an adverse shock, blocking or limiting its harmful effects. Resilience may also refer to the ability to change in response to a shock, either through limited adaptations or through more fundamental transformations, in ways that reduce or eliminate the danger it poses.[27] Whereas decoupling seeks to reduce interaction with China, efforts to boost resilience strive to limit the dangers that accompany such interaction.

There are several ways in which the United States and its partners can grow more resilient as China emerges as a technology power. The first is to become more capable of repelling or neutralising China's attempts to acquire advanced technologies through illicit means. There is much work to be done on this front, on both the national and international levels.[28] It is especially important that governments work together to improve protection for the most inviting targets. These include start-up firms, which frequently focus on cutting-edge technologies but lack the resources to invest adequately in security. While the US–EU Trade and Technology Council has taken some initial steps in this regard, more robust efforts are required. More generally, there is a clear need for much greater cyber-security expertise than currently exists: by one estimate, the world had 4.7 million cyber-security professionals in 2022, but it needed 3.4m more.[29]

While China-based actors are active practitioners of cyber espionage, China does have a role to play in bolstering cyber security. As noted, academic collaboration on defensive measures should be welcomed. In addition, software companies routinely compensate cyber-security researchers who identify and report vulnerabilities in their products. A study of one leading platform for such exchanges found that 85% of the compensation provided by US firms in 2021 went to researchers from outside the United States, and that China accounted for a greater share (10%) than any other foreign country.[30] It is important to keep these streams of information flowing, especially since Chinese cyber-security researchers are now required to report vulnerabilities they identify to the government.

While strengthening the capability to absorb attacks is one way to build resilience, another involves adapting to change. China's emergence as an increasingly important player in high-tech supply chains could well increase its leverage over other countries, while also giving it a greater ability to shape how new technologies work. To mitigate these risks, the world's advanced democracies have stepped up efforts to invigorate their own innovation systems, and breathed new life into industrial policy in the process. In the United States, this was evident in the passage of two major pieces of legislation in August 2022. The $280bn CHIPS and Science Act included $52bn for the US semiconductor industry, while the Inflation Reduction Act offered tax incentives, grants and loan programmes for clean-energy technologies. More fundamental changes, involving closer ties between government and private industry, have been proposed.[31] The European Union, meanwhile, plans to invest €43bn in its own semiconductor industry, and additional measures are in the works.[32]

These efforts to energise national innovation systems need to be combined with more transformational efforts – in particular, closer cooperation among allies and partners. There should be more concerted initiatives to devise alternative supply chains or make existing ones more flexible. It is frequently noted, for example, that the concept of 'Open RAN' – for 'open radio access network' – has the potential to reduce the risk of dependence on Chinese suppliers (particularly Huawei) for advanced telecommunications networks. In essence, Open RAN involves disaggregating the hardware and software components of radio-access networks, allowing multiple suppliers to participate, and providing network operators with what could be a more flexible and less expensive system. Open RAN's potential to provide an alternative to Huawei has already prompted some support from the Japanese, United Kingdom and US governments.

Yet it is unclear whether Open RAN will live up to its billing. To date, the main body developing technical specifications for Open RAN has been the O-RAN Alliance, a multinational group including more than 300 firms and research institutions. Dozens of Chinese companies participate in the alliance, including the country's major mobile operators and several firms on the US Department of Commerce's Entity List, which subjects entities deemed to be working against American interests to strict licensing requirements. In the future, state-supported Chinese firms could become leading Open RAN suppliers, and some Chinese strategists reportedly see it as an opportunity to circumvent current restrictions on China's 5G vendors.[33] Open RAN also raises new security concerns due to the increased number of providers, components and interfaces, among other factors. In May 2022, an EU report stated that 'security has not featured at the forefront of the technical specifications development process of the O-RAN Alliance'.[34] While the United States and various partners have pledged to work together, it is uncertain whether effective cooperation will emerge.[35] Government financial support for Open RAN, meanwhile, remains limited. The $1.5bn promised by the US government in 2022, for example, is minuscule given the scale of the task.[36] If Open RAN is to become an attractive alternative, more determined government leadership will be needed.

In any case, the United States and its partners must look beyond Open RAN and develop cooperative mechanisms across a range of high-tech sectors. Some observers have proposed a formal alliance of 'techno-democracies' – a 'T10' or 'T12' – while others suggest a more versatile and inclusive set of 'agile alliances'.[37] The latter approach has prevailed thus far, with the United States pursuing several multilateral and bilateral dialogues involving the EU, India, Israel, Japan, South Korea, Taiwan and the UK, among other countries.

The key question is what these initiatives will ultimately do. Greater cooperation is needed on the promotion of cross-border data flows among trusted partners and the development of technical standards that reflect democratic values.[38] Perhaps the most difficult task, however, is generating cooperation on industrial policy. While renewed interest in high-tech leadership is laudable, there is a danger that the various initiatives now under way or in the works will devolve into duplicative and wasteful efforts to lead in critical technology sectors. It would be much more efficient – and realistic – for like-minded countries to coordinate, collaborate and draw on each other's respective strengths.

To date, progress on this front has been far too limited. The 'Chip 4 Alliance', involving Japan, South Korea, Taiwan and the United States, has been hampered by concerns about China's reaction and about the competitive balance between leading semiconductor firms. The US–EU Trade and Technology Council, in turn, has been troubled by disputes over

US subsidies and local content requirements, and has taken only tentative steps towards facilitating information-sharing about semiconductor subsidies and reducing barriers to collaboration in quantum technologies.

To make progress on this front, participating parties need to recognise the limits of what they can accomplish alone. Increased government capacity is also required. The US government, for example, currently lacks the institutional capacity to lead (or even follow) cross-border collaboration in high-tech industrial policy.[39] It also lacks sufficient technical expertise to identify national strengths, weaknesses and opportunities in high-tech sectors.[40] Rectifying these and other problems will take time, money and political persistence. There is also a need for restraint, since industrial policies can devolve into government micromanagement. Despite these challenges, the development of deeper collaboration among the United States and its partners could substantially boost their collective capacity for innovation, reducing the danger of dependence on China in the future.

*   *   *

The United States and its allies and partners have arrived at a critical crossroads in their relations with China – and with one another. To contend with the rise of China, they must not merely engage in some degree of targeted decoupling, but also greatly strengthen efforts to bolster their collective resilience. Such efforts should include measures to absorb threatening Chinese actions – including cyber-enabled espionage – and measures to adapt and transform in response to China's growing technological prowess. While this will require considerable acumen and effort on the part of the US and its partners, the search for resilience promises renewed solidarity and greater opportunities to sustain technological leadership in the future.

Acknowledgements

The author would like to thank Benjamin Herscovitch and Anthea Roberts for their feedback on an earlier version of this article. The standard caveats apply.

Notes

[1] Recent studies of technological innovation in China include Richard P. Appelbaum et al., *Innovation in China: Challenging the Global Science and Technology System* (Cambridge: Polity, 2018); Tai Ming Cheung, *Innovate to Dominate: The Rise of the Chinese Techno-security State* (Ithaca, NY: Cornell University Press, 2022); Xiaolan Fu, Jin Chen and Bruce McKern (eds), *The Oxford Handbook of China Innovation* (Oxford: Oxford University Press, 2021); Xue Lan, *Zhongguo Keji Fazhan and Yu Zhengce* [China's S&T development and policies] (Beijing: Shehui Kexue Wenxian Chubanshe, 2018); and Yutao Sun and Cong Cao, 'Planning for Science: China's "Grand Experiment" and Global Implications', *Humanities and Social Sciences Communications*, vol. 8, no. 1, September 2021, pp. 1–9. On China's challenges in particular, see Douglas B. Fuller, *Paper Tigers, Hidden Dragons: Firms and the Political Economy of China's Technological Development* (Oxford: Oxford University Press, 2016); and Andrew B. Kennedy, 'China's Rise as a Science Power: Rapid Progress, Emerging Reforms, and the Challenge of Illiberal Innovation', *Asian Survey*, vol. 59, no. 6, November/December 2019, pp. 1,022–43.

[2] Doug Fuller, 'As the Fog Lifts: Reflections on the Chip War's Impact After One Month – Chip Fabrication', China Tech Tales, 6 November 2022, https://chinatechtales.wordpress.com/2022/11/06/as-the-fog-lifts-reflections-on-the-chip-wars-impact-after-one-month-chip-fabrication/.

[3] See Jeanne Whalen, 'Expect More China-related Tech Crackdowns, U.S. Official Says', *Washington Post*, 27 October 2022, https://www.washingtonpost.com/technology/2022/10/27/expect-more-china-related-tech-crackdowns-us-official-says/.

[4] See Dan Wang, 'China's Sputnik Moment? How Washington Boosted Beijing's Quest for Tech Dominance', *Foreign Affairs*, 29 July 2021, https://www.foreignaffairs.com/articles/united-states/2021-07-29/chinas-sputnik-moment.

[5] Olaf Scholz, 'The Global *Zeitenwende*: How to Avoid a New Cold War in a Multipolar Era', *Foreign Affairs*, vol. 102, no. 1, January/February 2023, pp. 22–38.

[6] See Anthea Roberts, 'Risk, Reward and Resilience: The Triple R Framework', Working Paper, Social Science Research Network, 14 September 2022, https://papers.ssrn.com/sol3/papers.cfm?abstract_id=4204026.

[7] See Tai Ming Cheung and Bates Gill, 'Trade Versus Security: How Countries Balance Technology Transfers with China', *Journal of East Asian Studies*, vol. 13, no. 3, September–December 2013, pp. 443–56; and Hugo Meijer, *Trading with the Enemy: The Making of US Export Control Policy Toward the People's Republic of China* (Oxford: Oxford University Press, 2016).

[8] See Cheung, *Innovate to Dominate*, pp. 115–16.

[9] See Zach Dorfman, 'Tech Giants Are Giving China a Vital Edge in Espionage', *Foreign Policy*, 23

December 2020, https://foreignpolicy.com/2020/12/23/china-tech-giants-process-stolen-data-spy-agencies/.

10 See Jean-Pierre Cabestan, 'The State and Digital Society in China: Big Brother Xi Is Watching You!', in Chien-wen Kou and Benjamin Hillman (eds), *Political and Social Control in the PRC: The Consolidation of Authoritarian Rule in Xi's China* (Canberra: ANU Press, forthcoming); and Willem Gravett, 'Digital Coloniser? China and Artificial Intelligence in Africa', *Survival*, vol. 62, no. 6, December 2020–January 2021, pp. 153–78.

11 See Jingyang Huang and Kellee S. Tsai, 'Securing Authoritarian Capitalism in the Digital Age: The Political Economy of Surveillance in China', *China Journal*, vol. 88, no. 1, July 2022, pp. 2–28.

12 See Adam Kozy, 'Testimony Before the U.S.–China Economic and Security Review Commission Hearing on "China's Cyber Capabilities: Warfare, Espionage, and Implications for the United States"', 17 February 2022, https://www.uscc.gov/sites/default/files/2022-02/Adam_Kozy_Testimony.pdf.

13 See Kelli Vanderlee, 'China's Capabilities for State-sponsored Cyber Espionage', testimony before the US–China Economic and Security Review Commission, 17 February 2022, https://www.uscc.gov/sites/default/files/2022-02/Kelli_Vanderlee_Testimony.pdf.

14 The leverage China derives from its market power is quite conditional and should not be overstated. See Victor Ferguson, Scott Waldron and Darren J. Lim, 'Market Adjustments to Import Sanctions: Lessons from Chinese Restrictions on Australian Trade, 2020–21', *Review of International Political Economy*, July 2022, https://www.tandfonline/doi/full/10.1080/09692290.2022.2090019.

15 See John Seaman et al. (eds), 'Dependence in Europe's Relations with China: Weighing Perceptions and Reality', European Think-tank Network on China, April 2022, https://merics.org/sites/default/files/2022-04/etnc_2022_report.pdf. In late 2022, Finnish Prime Minister Sanna Marin publicly warned that Europe should avoid becoming 'dependent on China and other authoritarian countries' for new technologies. 'Europe Is Too Dependent on China for Technologies, Finland's PM Says', Reuters, 17 November 2022, https://www.reuters.com/technology/europe-is-too-dependent-china-technologies-finlands-pm-says-2022-11-17/.

16 National Science Foundation, 'Doctorate Recipients from U.S. Universities', 2021, https://ncses.nsf.gov/pubs/nsf23300/.

17 See Andrew B. Kennedy and David L. Dwyer, 'The Stakes in Decoupling Discovery: China's Role in Transnational Innovation', *Pacific Review*, vol. 35, no. 1, 2022, pp. 147–71.

18 See Jenny J. Lee and John P. Haupt, 'Winners and Losers in US–China Scientific Research Collaborations', *Higher Education*, vol. 80, no. 1, July 2020, pp. 57–74. See also Nature, 'Connected World: Patterns of International Collaboration Captured by the Nature Index', https://www.nature.com/nature-index/country-outputs/collaboration-graph/.

19 See Nature, 'Nature Index', https://www.nature.com/nature-index/.

20 Holly Chik, 'China Makes Big Leap Forward in Basic Research Spending', *South China Morning Post*, 31 August 2022, https://www.scmp.com/news/china/science/article/3190874/china-makes-big-leap-forward-basic-research-spending.

21 See Valerie J. Karplus, M. Granger Morgan and David G. Victor, 'Finding Safe Zones for Science', *Issues in Science and Technology*, vol. 38, no. 1, Fall 2021, pp. 76–81.

22 See Dakota Cary, 'Testimony Before the U.S.–China Economic and Security Review Commission on "China's Cyber Capabilities: Warfare, Espionage and Implications for the United States"', 17 February 2022, https://cset.georgetown.edu/wp-content/uploads/Testimony-before-U.S.-China-Economic-and-Security-Review-Commission-Dakota-Cary.pdf.

23 See Lee G. Branstetter, Britta Glennon and J. Bradford Jensen, *The Rise of Global Innovation by US Multinationals Poses Risks and Opportunities* (Washington DC: Peterson Institute, 2021), pp. 11–13.

24 See Dan Mihalascu, 'Tesla China Announces R&D Center Is Complete, Teases Tesla Bot', InsideEVs, 26 October 2021, https://insideevs.com/news/543312/tesla-completes-shanghai-research-center/.

25 See Christopher A. Thomas and Xander Wu, 'How Global Tech Executives View U.S.–China Tech Competition', Brookings Institution, 25 February 2021, https://www.brookings.edu/techstream/how-global-tech-executives-view-u-s-china-tech-competition/; and AmCham China, *2022 China Business Climate Survey Report* (Beijing: AmCham China, 2022).

26 See Philippe Bourbeau, 'Resilience and International Politics: Premises, Debates, Agenda', *International Studies Review*, vol. 17, no. 3, September 2015, pp. 374–95.

27 See Roberts, 'Risk, Reward and Resilience'.

28 See Adam Segal and Gordon M. Goldstein, *Confronting Reality in Cyberspace: Foreign Policy for a Fragmented Internet* (New York: Council on Foreign Relations, 2022).

29 (ISC)2, '(ISC)² Cybersecurity Workforce Study 2022', p. 3, https://www.isc2.org//-/media/ISC2/Research/2022-WorkForce-Study/ISC2-Cybersecurity-Workforce-Study.ashx.

30 See Cary, 'Testimony Before the U.S.–China Economic and Security Review Commission on "China's Cyber Capabilities: Warfare, Espionage and Implications for the United States"'.

31 See, for example, David C. Gompert, 'Spin-on: How the US Can Meet China's Technological Challenge', *Survival*, vol. 62, no. 3, June–July 2020, pp. 115–30.

32 Jonathan Packroff and Nikolaus J. Kurmayer, 'Berlin Proclaims (European) "Year of Industrial Policy"', Euractiv, 29 November 2022, https://www.euractiv.com/section/economy-jobs/news/berlin-proclaims-european-year-of-industrial-policy/.

33 See Tim Rühlig and Jan-Peter Kleinhans, 'The False Promise of Open RAN', German Council on Foreign Relations, August 2022, pp. 12–13,

https://dgap.org/system/files/article_
pdfs/DPC-Open%20RAN%20-%20
FULL%20REPORT%20-%20FINAL.pdf.

34 EU NIS Cooperation Group, 'Report
on the Cybersecurity of Open
RAN', 11 May 2022, p. 9, https://
d110erj1750600.cloudfront.net/wp-
content/uploads/2022/05/11160610/
OPEN.pdf.

35 See Alexandra Seymour and Martijn
Rasser, 'Better Together: How the
Quad Countries Can Operationalise
5G Security', Observer Research
Foundation, December 2022, https://
www.orfonline.org/wp-content/
uploads/2022/12/ORF_Report_
Chrome-Dot-Network.pdf.

36 Caroline Gabriel, 'CHIPS Act's $1.5bn
Is a Drop in the Ocean for Open
RAN', Rethink Technology Research,
2 August 2022, https://rethinkresearch.
biz/articles/chips-acts-1-5bn-is-a-drop-
in-the-ocean-for-open-ran/.

37 Jared Cohen and Richard Fontaine,
'Uniting the Techno-democracies: How
to Build Digital Cooperation', *Foreign
Affairs*, vol. 99, no. 6, November/
December 2020, pp. 112–22; and

Andrew Imbrie et al., 'Agile Alliances:
How the United States and Its Allies
Can Deliver a Democratic Way of AI',
Center for Security and Emerging
Technology, February 2020.

38 See Matthew P. Goodman and Brooke
Roberts, 'Toward a T12: Putting Allied
Technology Cooperation into Practice',
Center for Strategic and International
Studies, 13 October 2021, https://csis-
website-prod.s3.amazonaws.com/
s3fs-public/publication/211013_
Goodman_Toward_T12.pdf?gPeOoA
p9ER7mdhXQW7OWYxqga_s133l.

39 See Bruce R. Guile et al., 'Democracies
Must Coordinate Industrial Policies
to Rebuild Economic Security', *Issues
in Science and Technology*, 14 April
2022, https://issues.org/coordinate-
industrial-policies-democracies-
economic-security-guile-tyson/.

40 See Erica R.H. Fuchs, 'Building the
Analytic Capacity to Support Critical
Technology Strategy', Brookings
Institution, 28 September 2022,
https://www.brookings.edu/research/
building-the-analytic-capacity-to-
support-critical-technology-strategy/.

Review Essay

Kissinger and Monnet: Realpolitik and Interdependence in World Affairs

Cesare Merlini

Leadership: Six Studies in World Strategy
Henry Kissinger. London and New York: Allen Lane and Penguin Press, 2022. £25.00/$36.00. 528 pp.

World Order
Henry Kissinger. London and New York: Penguin Books, 2015. £10.99/$20.00. 432 pp.

Jean Monnet: The First Statesman of Interdependence
François Duchêne. New York: W. W. Norton & Co., 1994. Out of print. 480 pp.

Henry Kissinger, at nearly 100, has produced yet another book. *Leadership: Six Studies in World Strategy* starts with a definition: 'Leaders think and act at the intersection of two axes: the first, between the past and the future; the second, between the abiding values and aspirations of those they lead' (p. xv). The six leaders he examines are Konrad Adenauer, Charles de Gaulle, Richard Nixon, Anwar Sadat, Lee Kuan Yew and Margaret Thatcher. 'Each of the six leaders', says Kissinger, 'in his or her way, passed through the fiery furnace of the "Second Thirty Years' War" – that is, the series of destructive conflicts stretching from the beginning of the First World War in August 1914

Cesare Merlini was director and then president of the Italian Institute of International Affairs from 1970 to 2001 and a non-resident senior fellow at the Brookings Institution from 2004 to 2016.

Survival | vol. 65 no. 1 | February–March 2023 | pp. 129–140   https://doi.org/10.1080/00396338.2023.2172860

to the end of the Second World War in September 1945.' That war, in his view, 'challenged the entire international system to overcome disillusionment in Europe and poverty in much of the rest of the world with new principles of order' (p. xix). The book has many interesting passages, often made lively by the personal involvement of the author, but it does not focus on the episodes in which he critically steered American foreign policy: the end of the Vietnam War, Cold War detente and the United States' opening to China.

Kissinger himself, of course, has not been a leader or a politician. He was rather a shaper of events that have made history and left an imprint. If he has any European counterpart, it might be Jean Monnet. The juxtaposition of their political and cultural legacies may help in interpreting the current phase of history.

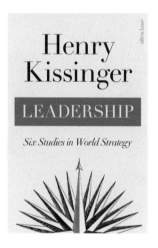

Two stories

Jean Monnet was born in Cognac, France, in 1888 to a wealthy family of producers of the famous brandy. At the start of the First World War, he was dismissed from military service for health reasons, but soon served as a civilian logistician for the French army and then was involved in the negotiations of the Versailles peace conference, as well as in the initial operations of the League of Nations. Back in the business world but frequently involved in international dealings, Monnet travelled the world during the 1920s and 1930s, and became familiar with American elites, including Franklin Delano Roosevelt. He also spent a year in China, where he met with Chinese premier Chiang Kai-shek. During the Second World War, Monnet operated as a liaison between the Allies and the French Resistance, occasionally travelling to London and Algiers, where he became acquainted with Charles de Gaulle. According to his biographer, François Duchêne, at a meeting with de Gaulle and others 'Monnet laid out his ideas of a Europe united on terms of equality among its members. It should be "a single economic entity with free trade" ... De Gaulle was sceptical: "After a war such as this, it is hard to see French and Germans belonging together to an economic union"' (p. 127).[1]

After 1945, Monnet moved to Paris and played a prominent role in the French reconstruction process. In view of the urgent need for coal and steel, he drafted the Schuman Plan for a European body in charge of pooling these two strategic resources. This would take shape, in 1951, as the European Coal and Steel Community, including Belgium, France, Italy, Luxembourg, the Netherlands and West Germany, and operating under a High Authority chaired by Monnet.

With the purpose of sharing sovereignty in the field of security, he also came up with the idea of the European Defence Community, in the form of a treaty signed by the same six countries. In 1954, however, the French National Assembly declined to ratify it, thanks to a coalition of communists and Gaullists. Monnet thereupon set up a private Action Committee, made up of political and trade-union leaders of the various countries, to promote two new projects: the European Economic Community (EEC) and Euratom. Both entered into effect on New Year's Day 1958. But de Gaulle, upon returning to power – first as prime minister and then, under a new constitution, as president – did his best to marginalise them while signing the bilateral Franco-German treaty with Adenauer and rejecting the United Kingdom's application to join the EEC. Yet the European institutions did endure, outliving de Gaulle and confirming Monnet's famous declaration that 'Europe will be forged in crises, and will be the sum of the solutions adopted for those crises'.[2]

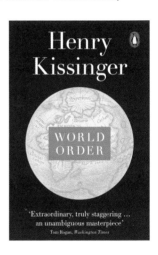

Having new solutions in mind, Monnet revived the idea of a European Reserve Fund, a precursor of the euro. He also devised the scheme for regular meetings of the heads of EEC member governments – the seed of intergovernmentalism in the integration process – while the entry of Denmark, Ireland and the UK into the community started the process of enlargement. Monnet spent the last years of his life writing his memoirs, his only book, and passed away in 1979.

Kissinger belongs to the next generation. Born in 1923 with the name of Heinz in a small city of Bavaria, his Jewish family fled to America in 1938, eventually settling into a modest life in New York City, sustained mainly by what his mother brought in as a cook and pastry chef. Heinz became Henry, enlisted in the US Army when the United States entered the Second World War, and became an American citizen. Towards the end of the war, he served in Germany as an interpreter.

After leaving military service, Kissinger enrolled at Harvard University, where he eventually received his PhD on the basis of a dissertation – now famous for shaping his thinking and statesmanship – titled 'Peace, Legitimacy and Equilibrium: A Study of the Statesmanship of Castlereagh and Metternich'. He stayed at the university to teach, becoming a full professor and initiating and running the influential Harvard International Seminar. He also became a foreign-policy consultant for various administrations, both Republican and Democratic. When Nixon was elected president in 1968, he asked Kissinger to be his national security advisor and later, for a time simultaneously, his secretary of state. He continued to serve in the latter position under Nixon's successor, Gerald R. Ford.

Kissinger's eight years as a cabinet-level official were extraordinarily eventful ones in world affairs and American foreign policy. During that period, the triangular strategic relationship that evolved among Washington, Moscow and Beijing, and the arduous termination of the Vietnam War, were driven substantially by Kissinger's intellectual approach – that is, realpolitik. After leaving the State Department, Kissinger returned to academia and established a political-consulting firm available to political leaders, including more than one president, and wealthy private clients.

Two approaches

The word 'order' and the word 'system' are often used interchangeably by scholars to describe the complex of international relations. The *Oxford English Dictionary*, however, associates the former with 'rank' and the latter with a 'set of things connected'. Under these definitions, 'order' best fits Kissinger's intellectual approach, 'system' Monnet's.

Order appears to be statecraft's primary objective in a world marked by multipolarity and power hierarchies among sovereign states. A system is more in line with a world distinguished by interdependence among states through effective equality, multilateralism and, ideally, integration. Order is fragile because it is subject to unilateralism and hegemony by dominant powers and vulnerable to disruption by the less powerful. A system is fragile because it is at odds with unrestrained sovereignty and nationalism.

'No truly global "world order" ever existed', admits Kissinger the historian in *World Order*. 'What passes for order in our time was devised in Western Europe nearly four centuries ago, at a peace conference in the German region of Westphalia, conducted without the involvement or even the awareness of most other continents or civilizations' (pp. 2–3). He is referring to the Peace of Westphalia, at the end of the first Thirty Years War in 1648, that remains the baseline source of order now. Its strength is 'its procedural – that is, value neutral – nature'. Its weakness is that it provides no 'sense of direction' or 'answer to the problem of how to generate legitimacy' (p. 363).

Then, says Kissinger the thinker, 'in building a world order, a key question concerns the substance of its unifying principles – in which resides a cardinal distinction between Western and non-Western approaches to order' (p. 363). Regarding the latter, 'Confucianism ordered the world into tributaries in hierarchy defined by approximations of Chinese culture. Islam divided the world order into a world of peace, that of Islam, and a world of war, inhabited by unbelievers.' The consequence, he says, 'is not simply a multipolarity of power but a world of increasingly contradictory realities' (p. 365).

'So, where do we go from here?' asks Kissinger the strategist. 'A reassessment of the concept of balance of power is in order' (p. 371) is his programmatic answer. 'A world order of states affirming individual dignity and participatory governance, and cooperating internationally in accordance with agreed-upon rules can be our hope and should be our inspiration' (p. 372). Is there any role for Europe to provide such inspiration? Not really, it seems. 'Europe has set out to depart from the state system it designed and to transcend it through a concept of pooled sovereignty', but 'having downgraded its military capacities Europe has little scope to respond when universal norms are flouted' (p. 7).

The concept of pooled sovereignty brings us to Monnet and his evaluation of the state system Europe itself had designed. Per Duchêne, Monnet told the first session of the Common Assembly of the European Coal and Steel Community – the forerunner to the EEC – in 1952: 'When one looks back a little on the past fifty, seventy-five or hundred years, and one sees the extraordinary disaster the Europeans have brought upon themselves, one is literally aghast. Yet the reason is simple. It is that each country pursued its destiny, or what it thought its destiny, by applying its own rules' (p. 364).

'If the destructiveness of international politics was to be outgrown', writes Duchêne, 'a structure had to be built up to induce people to take a "common view"' (p. 365). He cites Monnet's point that a common effort implies common goals, but also requires delegating sovereignty to institutions shared by all partners, big and small, on an equal basis. The issues of sovereignty and equality became especially controversial in France during the debate about ratification of the treaty establishing the European Defence Community. Its rejection was a major source of Kissinger's scepticism regarding the possible role of an integrated Europe in the neo-Westphalian order he envisaged.

Monnet, however, was not a federalist. While he respected Altiero Spinelli, the Italian founder of the European Federalist Movement, and later included him in the Action Committee, Monnet thought Europe was too diverse to federate along the lines of the United States. Indeed, European federalists regarded his plan for heads of member governments to meet regularly as a diminution of the supranational role of the common institutions.

Monnet's 'common effort' was not limited to the six founders of the first communities. He had been pursuing Britain's involvement in the European project from the start, provided London could accept a supranational authority with independent powers. Nor was his approach about Europe only. On the strength of his pre-1945 American acquaintances and the establishment of NATO, which he supported, Monnet envisaged a partnership of equals between the United States and the 'newly uniting states of Europe' (p. 384). This was anathema to de Gaulle but inspiration to, among others, John F. Kennedy.

Finally, Monnet was not a Cold War zealot. According to Duchêne, in a speech Monnet gave when receiving an honorary degree from Dartmouth College in 1961, he said that 'when it has become evident to everyone that it is impossible to divide the West … Mr Khrushchev or his successor will accept the facts. The conditions will then exist at last for transforming so-called peaceful coexistence into genuine peace' (p. 380). A decade or so later one such successor, Leonid Brezhnev, in fact changed the Soviet character-isation of the EEC from capitalist conspiracy to the model to consider in setting up the Comecon, the common market of the communist bloc.

Monnet's conviction was that the community framework could be applied universally, and fledgling regional organisations such as Mercosur in Latin America seemed to give substance to the idea. He was a strong supporter of the more ambitious United Nations, in particular its efforts to manage the new threat of nuclear war. He originally hoped that Euratom would comprehensively control the use of uranium by the six member countries under the auspices of the International Atomic Energy Agency, a UN organisation, though its writ was ultimately confined to civilian nuclear power, and with severe limitations.

Two legacies and the Russia–Ukraine war

Monnet died long before the fall of the Berlin Wall and the reunification of Germany. Had he lived longer, it is unlikely that he would have associated himself with French president François Mitterrand and British prime minis-ter Margaret Thatcher's maladroit attempts to resist German reunification. He would have trusted the framework of a unifying Europe as a stabilising alternative to abject nationalism.

Following the end of the Cold War, the European Union's enlargement sharply accelerated as the organisation absorbed new members from the east that had been neutral states or members of the Warsaw Pact. By 2013, the community of six had become a union of 28. The prospect of making war impossible among members of a single economic entity that shared the values of freedom and democracy had become a reality. The process of 'deepening' proved less salutary. While the Maastricht Treaty codified Monnet's suggestion of joining the leaders of the member states through the European Council, the subsequent effort to devise a workable constitu-tion died by way of a referendum in France. The alternative – the Lisbon Treaty signed in 2007 – strengthened the EU's intergovernmental core at the expense of its communitarian spirit.[3]

The drift towards intergovernmentalism was subtly consistent with a global trend opaquely described as the 'return of the states'. Sinisterly, it subsumed the rise of nationalism and authoritarianism. In a more positive light, it connoted a new prominence for geopolitics and realpolitik in an increasingly multipolar world, squaring with the world order contemplated by Kissinger.

According to him, writing in *World Order*, the Soviet Union had been 'a challenge to the Westphalian state system' (p. 327). Thus, its collapse and the emergence of China following the consecration of the United States as the sole superpower was a gilded opportunity for a new Westphalian order to take shape, duly updated to account for such epochal new factors as nuclear deterrence and information technology, and run by a revised and possibly more capable concert of powers. This was the alternative to the US-led liberal-international system centred on global interdependence through multilateralism and the rule of law. The Kissingerian scheme, however, faced challenges. They came mainly from largely American 'neo-conservatives' who countenanced what Francis Fukuyama called 'the end of history' and, especially after 9/11, advocated a more unilateral and aggressive foreign policy under such broad slogans as 'spreading democracy' and 'war on terror', which resulted in the 'endless wars' in Afghanistan and Iraq. Though he initially supported these interventions, Kissinger came to assess in *World Order* that 'in only one of the five wars America fought after World War II, the first Gulf War under President George H. W. Bush, did America achieve the goals it had put forward for entering it without intense domestic division' (p. 328).

Inspired by the seventeenth- and eighteenth-century tsar Peter the Great, Russian President Vladimir Putin has restored attention to the Old Continent, claiming Russian ancestral sovereignty over several territories on its western borders – including, most egregiously, Ukraine. In 2008, when the George W. Bush administration insisted that the doors to NATO be left open to Georgia and Ukraine, Kissinger was critical. He thought, correctly, that this dispensation needlessly antagonised a Kremlin whose contribution to the new concert of powers was crucial. He shared the soft reaction of the United States under Barack Obama, Germany under Angela Merkel and France under François Hollande to Russia's military seizure of Crimea, thereby establishing a *droit de regard* over Ukraine's eastern provinces. But Kissinger went further. In spring 2017, during Donald Trump's fraught and erratic presidency, Kissinger said publicly that Putin was not a Hitler and would not wage a policy of conquest, as he was simply after restoring the dignity of his country, and that negotiations remained imperative.

Putin, of course, did implement a 'policy of conquest' less than five years later, invading Ukraine, on 24 February 2022. 'Only powerful and sovereign states can have their say in this emerging world order', he explained in a speech a few months later.[4] Kissinger had to admit that he 'would have not predicted an attack of the magnitude of taking over a recognised country', adding that 'we are not going back to the previous relationship [with Russia]'. At the same time, realpolitik drove him to deem it 'unwise to take an adversarial position to two adversaries [China and Russia] in a way that drives them together'.[5]

The European project has shown remarkable resilience

Putin's 'special military operation' has been a strategic failure, but it has also devastated the people of Ukraine. Although the war's outcome is uncertain, it has taken Europe to a place it had not been since 1945, and confirmed the fragility of a world order based on power relations among sovereign states. Significantly, when Russia invaded, several commentators referred to the precedent of 1914, when European nations 'sleepwalked' into the First World War, having relied on the inheritance of Westphalia updated by the Congress of Vienna.

The other approach – multilateralism and the rule of law aiming towards global interdependence – has had shortcomings, too. Its advocates were unable to capitalise on the extraordinary opportunity presented by the end of the Cold War. Over the course of the Ukraine crisis, the Organization for Security and Co-operation in Europe, the civilian regional body putatively tasked with managing European security, has been largely invisible, while the UN, the global body so tasked, has been marginal, offering little more than the General Assembly's non-binding resolution condemning Russia.

At the same time, the European project has shown remarkable resilience. The war has hardened Ukraine's aspiration to join the EU. Moreover, the

Union's cohesion in supporting the country under attack by extending funds, hosting refugees and supplying weapons has not only exceeded expectations but also energised the debate about the political and security dimensions of European integration.

*   *   *

Martin Wolf notes that 'geopolitics is the biggest threat to globalisation'.[6] The return of the states has not yet obliterated global trade and value chains, but economic measures dictated by perceived national interests and geopolitical imperatives, including protectionism, repatriation and sanctions, have impaired them. 'Countries', observes Mark Leonard, 'are waging conflicts by manipulating the very things that link them together: connections.'[7] Environmental deterioration is the most critical challenge of global governance, yet the near-impasse at the UN-sponsored conference on global warming shows how difficult it is to reconcile common effort with realpolitik.[8]

On trade, migration, connectivity, public health and climate change, the EU appears to be a step ahead of national actors in devising strategies, but lagging in capacity to steer them. The current adverse trends in world affairs do not augur well for applying and expanding the multilateral approach. Instead, those trends seem to point at a potential reprise of the state of affairs preceding what Kissinger considers to be the 'Second Thirty Years' War'. Averting such a scenario calls for new statesmen of interdependence like Jean Monnet.

Notes

[1] François Duchêne was director of the IISS from 1969 to 1974.

[2] Jean Monnet, *Memoirs* (Garden City, NY: Doubleday, 1978), p. 417.

[3] For an excellent analysis of the process, see Sergio Fabbrini, 'Who Holds the Elephant to Account? Executive Power Political Accountability in the EU', *Journal of European Integration*, vol. 43, no. 8, April 2021, pp. 923–38.

[4] See President of Russia, 'St Petersburg International Economic Forum Plenary Session', 17 June 2022, http://en.kremlin.ru/events/president/news/68669.

[5] '"We Are Now Living in a Totally New Era" – Henry Kissinger', interview conducted by Edward

Luce, *Financial Times*, 9 May 2022, https://www.ft.com/content/cd88912d-506a-41d4-b38f-0c37cb7f0e2f.

6   Martin Wolf, 'Geopolitics Is the Biggest Threat to Globalisation', *Financial Times*, 1 November 2022, https://www.ft.com/content/8954a5f8-8f03-4044-8401-f1efefe9791b.

7   Mark Leonard, *The Age of Unpeace: How Connectivity Causes Conflict* (London: Penguin Books, 2021).

8   See Anatol Lieven, 'Climate Change and the State: A Case for Environmental Realism', *Survival*, vol. 62, no. 2, April–May 2020, pp. 7–26.

Gambling the World: The Cuban Missile Crisis Revisited

Russell Crandall

Nuclear Folly: A New History of the Cuban Missile Crisis
Serhii Plokhy. London: Allen Lane, 2021. £25.00. 444 pp.

On 21 September 2022, Russian President Vladimir Putin issued a stern warning during his announcement of a partial mobilisation to reinforce the Russian invasion of Ukraine. 'In the event of a threat to the territorial integrity of our country and to defend Russia and our people, we will certainly make use of all weapon systems available to us', Putin said. 'This is not a bluff.'[1] A few days later, he suggested that the United States had set a 'precedent' by using nuclear weapons against Hiroshima and Nagasaki in the Second World War.[2] On 27 September, Dmitry Medvedev, deputy chairman of Russia's Security Council, former president and long-time Putin stooge, doubled down, saying that the West would not interfere in Ukraine even if Russia were 'forced to use the most fearsome weapon against the Ukrainian regime', because the 'demagogues across the ocean and in Europe are not going to die in a nuclear apocalypse'.[3]

Western leaders immediately condemned these comments, with US National Security Advisor Jake Sullivan saying that Washington had promised 'catastrophic consequences' if Moscow used nuclear weapons,[4] and retired general and former CIA director David Petraeus predicting that

Russell Crandall is a professor of American foreign policy and international politics at Davidson College in North Carolina, and a contributing editor to *Survival*. His latest books are *Drugs and Thugs: The History and Future of America's War on Drugs* (Yale University Press, 2020) and, with Britta Crandall, *"Our Hemisphere"?: The United States in Latin America, from 1776 to the Twenty-first Century* (Yale University Press, 2021).

Survival | vol. 65 no. 1 | February–March 2023 | pp. 141–154   https://doi.org/10.1080/00396338.2023.2172863

NATO would destroy all Russian troops and equipment in Ukraine (including in Crimea) and sink its entire Black Sea Fleet if Russia used a nuclear weapon.[5] At a Democratic fundraiser on 6 October, US President Joe Biden said that 'we have not faced the prospect of Armageddon since Kennedy and the Cuban Missile Crisis … I don't think there's any such thing as the ability to easily [use] a tactical nuclear weapon and not end up with Armageddon.'[6]

Dismantling the Kennedy myth

The current crisis makes Serhii Plokhy's new book, *Nuclear Folly: A New History of the Cuban Missile Crisis*, particularly timely, although discussion of the Cuban Missile Crisis has rarely waned over the past six decades. Indeed, the Cuban stand-off is one of the most documented and consulted

episodes of global diplomacy in history, spawning countless books, articles, documentaries and a couple of films, including 2000's *Thirteen Days*. Plokhy is of the opinion that, out of this profusion of evidence and arguments, a conventional myth has emerged, at least in the United States. According to this legend, a steely and brilliant John F. Kennedy – and his equally brilliant advisers – used an iterative, often fraught but ultimately successful decision-making process to best their Soviet adversary, led by Nikita Khrushchev.

It is debateable how unconventional this take really is; as noted below, others have tackled the myth rather comprehensively. Plokhy does argue, however, that 'major gaps' remain in our understanding of the episode, especially when we consider it from a more global and less Washington-centric perspective (p. xv). Plokhy's research draws heavily on Soviet sources and argues that both sides got things 'wrong, sometimes impossibly, catastrophically wrong', due to conflicting political agendas; misunderstandings of the adversary's geopolitical methods and goals; faulty intelligence; and cultural ignorance (p. xvii). In his assessment, both Kennedy and Khrushchev were equally clumsy.

The author sets the scene by outlining the geopolitical contours of the Cold War in the early 1960s. On the US side, Kennedy, a youthful Democrat, entered office on 20 January 1961, urging idealism and democracy: 'We shall pay any price, bear any burden, meet any hardship, support any friend, oppose any foe to assure the survival and success of liberty.'[7] Only a few months later, however, Kennedy's foreign policy would suffer a humiliating setback at the Bay of Pigs in Cuba. The fiasco was to leave Kennedy with a feeling of political impotence, especially vis-à-vis Khrushchev, and he began to obsess over Fidel Castro's communist regime. Robert Kennedy, then attorney general and brother of the president, strenuously pushed for *Operation Mongoose*, a CIA-implemented secret plot to bring about regime change in Cuba in late 1961.

Having written numerous books on the Soviet Union, Plokhy, a historian of Russia and Ukraine at Harvard University, is an especially astute guide to the climate of palace intrigue present during Khrushchev's time in the Kremlin, and the heightened internal tension resulting from US president Dwight Eisenhower's deployment of *Jupiter* medium-range ballistic missiles (MRBMs) equipped with 1.44-megaton nuclear warheads to Italy and Turkey (15 missiles each) in 1958 and 1959.[8] Given their 2,400-kilometre range, the missiles placed in Turkey directly threatened Moscow, a little over 2,000 km away. Rattled and furious, Khrushchev publicly protested in February 1961 about what he saw as a gratuitous nuclear escalation. Kennedy, in office for just under a month, ignored him.

At this point, as Plokhy explains, both Kennedy and Khrushchev knew full well that only the US possessed a sufficient number of intercontinental ballistic missiles (ICBMs) to annihilate its adversary, and Kennedy appeared ready to use them, stating that 'in some circumstances we must be prepared to use nuclear weapons at the start, come what may – a clear attack on Western Europe, for example' (pp. 54–5). While the president later retracted this statement, Khrushchev's anger was never assuaged.

To counter the imbalance in ICBMs (in 1961, the Soviet Union possessed only four such missiles), Khrushchev signed off on a programme to develop and deploy them from spring 1962, a plan that would inevitably take some time (Soviet ICBMs only became fully operational in the early 1970s). But Khrushchev had a stopgap solution: while the Soviet Union had nothing to counter the American ICBMs, it had no shortage of MRBMs and short-range ballistic missiles that could hit the continental US from Cuba. 'In addition to protecting Cuba [from a US invasion]', said the Soviet premier years later, 'our missiles would equalize what the West likes to call the "balance of power"' (p. 58). Plokhy cites an eyewitness's recollection of Khrushchev's rhetoric at a May 1962 meeting of the Presidium of the Central Committee: 'Since the Americans have already surrounded the Soviet Union with a ring of their military bases and multipurpose installations, we should pay them back in their own coin and give them a taste of their own medicine so that they find out for themselves how it feels to live as a target of nuclear arms' (p. 66). Not unreasonably, Khrushchev reckoned that the Americans would have to tolerate such a move, much as he had done in Europe, and calculated that Kennedy would be anxious to avoid war. In addition, Khrushchev was aware of the blowback Kennedy was facing from the Bay of Pigs and believed that, once burned, the president would be reluctant to try anything else in Cuba, leaving the island open for his gambit.

Khrushchev's 'half-baked idea' to protect Cuba and rattle Washington became a legitimate military operation almost overnight (p. 63). The Russian armed forces opted for a maximalist campaign that would establish a full-scale military base in Cuba along with 60 missiles equipped with 60 nuclear warheads. Even the name of the task force – the Group of Soviet Armed Forces in Cuba – paralleled that of the Group of Soviet Forces in East Germany, suggesting the Soviets were shifting the western military boundary of the Iron Curtain to the doorstep of the continental US. Complicating this already difficult logistical operation was Khrushchev's desire to keep it all secret.

Consulting Castro

Like Khrushchev, Castro firmly believed that if the Americans saw war with Cuba as a war with Moscow, there would never be a *yanqui* invasion of the island. Thus, Castro had pushed aggressively for a bilateral pact with Moscow that would guarantee Cuba's security along the lines of the Warsaw Pact or, even better, NATO's Article 5, whereby an attack against Cuba would be treated as an attack against the Soviet Union.

In July 1962, Sergey Biriuzov, a top Soviet nuclear official, told Castro that the Soviet Union was committed to protecting Cuba 'by all possible means' and was 'considering the question of installing medium-range nuclear weapons' (p. 68). All Fidel had to do was say yes to the operation. It was a stunning offer given that mere weeks before, Havana had been imploring Moscow to provide coastal anti-ship missiles for expected US attacks. Now, nuclear weapons were on the table. Biriuzov's diplomacy persuaded Castro to back the secret deployment, known as *Operation Anadyr*, even if the Cuban premier was dismayed about not being offered a collective-security pact.

Yet the deployment was to encounter numerous problems – both preventable and otherwise – from the get-go. Even before the Cuba phase began, more than 1,000 soldiers and 500 officers designated for deployment there were deemed unfit for the mission for myriad reasons. Making matters worse, many of the troops had been wrapping up their three-year terms of service, and morale plummeted once they realised that their return to civilian life had been indefinitely delayed. One sailor on the cargo ship *Orenburg* told his comrades that 'he had not taken an order to serve Fidel Castro and was going to Cuba under duress' (p. 93). A KGB officer on the same vessel commanded his informers to be on the lookout for officers and crew tempted to defect. When the ship sailed through the tight Bosporus Strait, all crew, including officers, were ordered inside, and armed guards patrolled the deck to forestall anyone trying to swim ashore.

More problems arose after the missiles had been safely delivered to the island, including Cuba's lack of sufficient natural cover, leaving the operation open to sightings by American spy flights. After arriving in Cuba in October, General Anatoly Gribkov, the operation's commander, blasted his country's 'strategic illiteracy' for having apparently assumed that palm groves would be sufficient (p. 70). Khrushchev's plan had been based on missiles that were literally too long to keep secret (p. 73). For their part, the Cubans were making a variety of demands regarding the missiles' installation on the island, such as where and how big the installations should be. Cuba's tropical heat and humidity also posed a major challenge to missile readiness.

A big surprise

As troublesome as these complications were, much bigger headaches were in store. Given that the Americans had, in July and August alone, detected more than three dozen cargo ships docking in Cuban ports, it was not a stretch for Washington to conclude that some sort of arms build-up was in the works. The Kennedy administration assessed, however, that this was intended to bolster Cuba's *defensive* capabilities. This tentative assessment was reinforced in late August when a U-2 spy plane took photographs revealing the existence of SA-2 surface-to-air missiles at eight different Cuban sites.[9] (For a host of reasons related to stealth, during *Operation Anadyr*'s initial phase over the summer, the Soviets prioritised the delivery and installation of anti-aircraft weapons over the missiles and warheads.) Still, there were some in Washington who thought the Soviets were up to something more. In late August, Kenneth B. Keating, a Republican senator from New York, publicly declared there was evidence (likely based on intelligence from Cuban exiles) of Soviet 'rocket installations' on the island, exhorting Kennedy to act.[10] Hawks like Robert Kennedy even urged an operation involving a faked Cuban attack on the US naval base at Guantanamo Bay.

Plokhy believes that Washington's discovery of the anti-aircraft defences did not set back Khrushchev's campaign, given that the Americans did not appear to be upset about them. On 4 September, John Kennedy publicly admonished Moscow not to place *offensive* weapons in Cuba, but remained silent about the defensive weaponry.[11] The anti-aircraft defences did complicate the business of gathering intelligence for American U-2 spy planes: fear of a plane being shot down and bad weather were key reasons why there were no flights for much of September. The White House was not aware when the first nuclear warheads arrived in Cuba during the first week of October. It wasn't until 14 October that a U-2 plane took pictures revealing that, amid the surface-to-air defences on Cuba, there were installations being constructed for MRBMs that would be capable of hitting most of the eastern US with nuclear warheads.

Opinion in Washington about how to respond to this discovery was mixed. The Pentagon's Joint Chiefs of Staff, as well as some civilians, recommended hitting the missile installations before a full-blown invasion, while

Robert Kennedy was 'even more radical', pushing for yet another regime-change operation, even if this provoked an outright war (p. 144). Plokhy's sensible take is that if the White House had decided to pre-emptively strike the ballistic-missile sites, the Soviets would likely have responded with nuclear weapons, possibly starting with tactical weapons before deciding whether to escalate to MRBMs. The nuclear war that the president 'was so desperate to avoid would have broken out almost immediately' if a strike plan had been implemented (p. 144).

After several intense rounds of deliberations, Kennedy opted for a more moderate course of action. This became the so-called 'quarantine' that the president announced to the American people on 22 October, telling them that it was necessary in the face of 'unmistakable evidence' of Soviet missiles in Cuba.[12] The quarantine's goal was to keep additional offensive weaponry from reaching the island. (U-2s had also discovered an intermediate-range-missile location by the time of the 22 October address.[13]) That same day, Kennedy sent a letter to Khrushchev stating that the US would never tolerate the transportation of offensive weapons to Cuba and demanding that Moscow remove the missile sites already there. The missive represented the first in a sequence of public and secret, direct and indirect communications between Washington and Moscow that would continue for the duration of the impasse.

In Plokhy's estimation, Washington's decision not to attack would have come as some relief to Khrushchev as it meant he did not have to use the tactical nukes. According to the author, 'for all the differences between the two men, and the misjudgments and misunderstandings that accompanied their search for the right decision, they both had something in common. They dreaded a nuclear war' (p. 171). Any relief would have been short-lived, as on 26 October – when resolution of the crisis appeared distant – US Strategic Air Command raised its Defense Readiness Condition (DEFCON) to Level 2, meaning that war was imminent. If a Soviet diplomat's recollection is to be believed, upon hearing about the DEFCON 2 status, Khrushchev 'shat his pants' (p. 194). That same day, he composed a rambling, pleading letter to Kennedy, writing that, 'if there is no intention to doom the world to the catastrophe of thermonuclear war, then let us not only relax the forces pulling on the ends of the rope, let us take measures to untie that knot. We are ready for this.'[14]

On 27 October, Khrushchev fired off another secret communication to the White House, this time indicating that any potential resolution had to entail the US pulling its *Jupiter* missiles from Turkey. That same day, a Soviet surface-to-air crew shot down a U-2 over Cuba, killing the pilot. Feeling out of options to break the deadlock, Kennedy and his team believed they would be ordering an attack against Cuba within a matter of days.

Jupiters in Turkey

Plokhy highlights how, time and again, the '*Jupiters* in Turkey' question arose in the White House, with the US president demonstrating a surprising lack of perspective. As the author puts it, 'Kennedy seemed oblivious to any parallel between the Soviet and American missiles' (p. 216). At one point Kennedy remarked that Khrushchev's gambit in Cuba was 'just as if we suddenly began to put a major number of MRBMs in Turkey. Now that'd be goddam dangerous, I would think.' One of his senior advisers had to remind the president that this is precisely what the US had done. 'Yeah, but it was five years ago', rejoined Kennedy.[15]

Plokhy notes that the White House's thinking on the *Jupiters* was influenced by the fact that Turkey was a member of NATO, meaning that the removal of the missiles might lead allied European capitals to conclude that the Americans were 'abandoning them to the Soviets' (p. 214). But Kennedy also understood that the *Jupiters* were strategically next to useless, since the Soviets would take them out pre-emptively in a general war. Balancing the options, Kennedy decided that he would accept the removal of the missiles as part of a bilateral deal, but only in private.

Thus, on 27 October, the US president decided to ignore Khrushchev's second message and respond only to the first, proposing a UN-observed removal of the Soviet missiles in return for the US not attacking. But he also sent his brother Robert to meet with Anatoly Dobrynin, the Soviet ambassador in Washington, to inform him that the president was planning to withdraw the *Jupiters* from Turkey. This concession could not be part of any public agreement, however, and the actual removal would take place at a later date. Nothing to this effect would be written down – the Soviets would have to take the Americans at their word.

So they did. Within hours of the Kennedy–Dobrynin meeting, Khrushchev publicly stated that his missiles would be withdrawn from Cuba in return for Kennedy's promise not to invade the island. With the crisis over, Khrushchev immediately shifted his attention to convincing his domestic constituency that he had in fact triumphed. 'This is not cowardice. It's a reserve position', he said, arguing that the US could be wiped out from Soviet soil (an unlikely proposition given the ICBMs deficit). Khrushchev's conundrum, Plokhy explains, was that he could not disclose why he had discarded his insistence that the *Jupiters* in Turkey be removed as a condition for the withdrawal of the Cuban missiles. As a result, many of those observing the crisis beyond the reach of Soviet propaganda thought that Kennedy had prevailed. Indeed, many within the Soviet apparatus held the same opinion. Over the next year or so, numerous senior Soviet officials came to see Khrushchev's leadership as 'mercurial' and 'idiotic', concluding that he had needlessly brought the Soviet Union – and the world – to the brink of a nuclear holocaust (p. 357). Upon voting to remove Khrushchev two years later, members of the Presidium broke into applause following a 'devastating critique' of the leader's myriad errors over Cuba (p. 357).

Equally critical was Castro, who had not been consulted or even notified about the bilateral deal (he learned of it from a US news outlet). Given how docile Eastern Bloc regimes were vis-à-vis Moscow, Khrushchev may have assumed that Castro would be a similarly submissive client, but if so, he was very much mistaken (p. 302). According to Plokhy, Castro 'considered himself to have been robbed not only of missiles and nuclear warheads that he already had on the island but also and more importantly, of his dignity as head of an independent country' (p. 301). For his part, Khrushchev was irate over what he perceived as Cuban ingratitude, since in his eyes he had secured Cuba's survival.

Relearning old lessons

Plokhy not unreasonably concludes that Khrushchev's gambit was a catastrophic, unnecessary blunder: 'The price that everyone – Americans, Cubans, and Soviets – paid for his adventurism turned out to be too high to justify his alleged successes' (p. 358). In the aftermath, the two sides agreed to establish a direct telephone connection – what became known as the 'hotline' – to try to overcome the confusion generated by the exchange of information and misinformation through direct and back channels simultaneously. The two superpowers also placed more emphasis on nuclear negotiations, culminating in the signing of the Limited Nuclear Test Ban Treaty in August 1963.[16]

Plokhy suggests that there are multiple parallels between US–Russian relations today and at the time of the Cuban Missile Crisis. Contemporary Russia, he thinks, is a 'revisionist power' much as it was in the 1950s and 1960s, when it was trying to foment global revolution, especially in what was then called the Third World. Another similarity is that dominion over nuclear weapons remains in the hands of just a few people, with the rest of the world dependent on their leadership and political skills, the soundness of their judgement and the strength of their nerve (p. 362). In October 1962, the globe was spared a nuclear war because both leaders viewed the prospect as intolerable.

But times have also changed. The momentum behind arms control has wavered in recent years: while New START was extended (at the last minute) until 2026, the US withdrew from the Intermediate-Range Nuclear Forces Treaty (INF Treaty) in 2019, citing Russian non-compliance. New technologies have increased the risks of future nuclear strikes, most conspicuously in the shape of hypersonic missiles, which travel so fast they may hit their target before an alarm can be raised. The development of nuclear technology by the so-called 'rogue' states Iran and North Korea has further challenged Cold War norms of deterrence and calculations of nuclear risk. For Plokhy, the 'psychological barrier' against nuclear-weapons use has been reduced, making 'nuclear confrontation more likely' (p. 362). He warns that the world has become 'more dangerous and unpredictable', and that humanity has 'unlearned the lessons of the past' – to 'survive in the current age, we must learn them anew' (p. xviii).

If there is a criticism to be made of this eminently readable Cold War history it is that, while promising an overdue yet vital international perspective on the events of October 1962, the author does not explicitly explain what is new in his account. Indeed, his central thesis closely echoes that of historian Michael Dobbs in his book *One Minute to Midnight* (2009), which also highlighted the flaws of the 'Kennedy myth'. As Dobbs wrote in the *New York Times* in 2012,

> there is now plenty of evidence that Kennedy – like Khrushchev – was a lot less steely-eyed than depicted in the initial accounts of the crisis, which were virtually dictated by the White House. Tape-recorded transcripts of White House debates and notes from participants show that Kennedy was prepared to make significant concessions, including a public trade of Soviet missiles in Cuba for American missiles in Turkey and possibly the surrender of the United States naval base at Guantánamo Bay.[17]

Another question for the author is how to weigh the respective performances of the two leaders: surely Kennedy's deliberative (albeit imperfect) approach entailed significantly less folly than Khrushchev's rash gamble on levelling the nuclear playing field? Did Kennedy really march from 'one mistake to the other', as the author posits (p. xvi)? Perhaps it was Robert Kennedy and his fellow hawks among the Pentagon brass who were foolish, reined in by a sober president? And is it possible that our understanding of Khrushchev's actions has been coloured by disaffected or vengeful Soviet officials distorting the narrative for their own political ends?

Plokhy's book demonstrates that the Cuban Missile Crisis remains instructive to every age, not because of the nature of its two chief protagonists but for the warning it provides about the dangers of misunderstandings. As Dobbs says, the risk of nuclear conflict during the Cuban Missile Crisis 'was not caused by a clash of wills. The real dangers arose from "the fog of war."'[18]

Notes

[1] President of Russia, 'Address by the President of the Russian Federation', 21 September 2022, http://en.kremlin.ru/events/president/news/69390. See also Robyn Dixon, Catherine Belton and Mary Ilyushina, 'Putin Drafts up to 300,000 Reservists, Backs Annexation Amid War Losses', *Washington Post*, 21 September 2022.

[2] President of Russia, 'Signing of Treaties on Accession of Donetsk and Lugansk People's Republics and

Zaporozhye and Kherson Regions to Russia', 30 September 2022, http://en.kremlin.ru/events/president/news/69465.

3   See 'NATO Won't Interfere if Russia Uses Nuke Weapons Against Ukrainian Aggression – Medvedev', TASS, 27 September 2022; and Tom Nichols, 'Russia's Nuclear Threats Are All Putin Has Left', *Atlantic*, 27 September 2022, https://www.theatlantic.com/newsletters/archive/2022/09/russias-nuclear-threats/671571/.

4   Edward Helmore, 'Jake Sullivan: US Will Act "Decisively" if Russia Uses Nuclear Weapons in Ukraine', *Guardian*, 25 September 2022.

5   Edward Helmore, 'Petraeus: US Would Destroy Russia's Troops if Putin Uses Nuclear Weapons in Ukraine', *Guardian*, 2 October 2022.

6   Nandita Bose, 'Biden Cites Cuban Missile Crisis in Describing Putin's Nuclear Threat', Reuters, 7 October 2022.

7   'President John F. Kennedy's Inaugural Address (1961)', available from the US National Archives, https://www.archives.gov/milestone-documents/president-john-f-kennedys-inaugural-address.

8   See Nur Bilge Criss, 'Strategic Nuclear Missiles in Turkey: The Jupiter Affair, 1959–1963', *Journal of Strategic Studies*, vol. 20, no. 3, 1997, pp. 97–122.

9   John T. Correll, 'Airpower and the Cuban Missile Crisis', *AIR FORCE Magazine*, August 2005, p. 79, https://media.defense.gov/2012/Jul/27/2001330167/-1/-1/0/0805U2.pdf.

10 *Ibid*.

11 See US Department of State, Office of the Historian, 'The Cuban Missile Crisis, October 1962', https://history.state.gov/milestones/1961-1968/cuban-missile-crisis.

12 John F. Kennedy, 'Address During the Cuban Missile Crisis', 22 October 1962, available from the John F. Kennedy Presidential Library and Museum, https://www.jfklibrary.org/learn/about-jfk/historic-speeches/address-during-the-cuban-missile-crisis.

13 See US Department of State, Office of the Historian, 'The Cuban Missile Crisis, October 1962'.

14 'Telegram from the Embassy in the Soviet Union to the Department of State', 26 October 1962, available from the US Department of State, Office of the Historian, https://history.state.gov/historicaldocuments/frus1961-63v06/d65.

15 See White House, 'Off the Record Meeting on Cuba', 16 October 1962, available from the John F. Kennedy Presidential Library and Museum, https://microsites.jfklibrary.org/cmc/oct16/doc3.html; and Criss, 'Strategic Nuclear Missiles in Turkey'.

16 See John F. Kennedy Presidential Library and Museum, 'Nuclear Test Ban Treaty', https://www.jfklibrary.org/learn/about-jfk/jfk-in-history/nuclear-test-ban-treaty.

17 Michael Dobbs, 'The Price of a 50-year Myth', *New York Times*, 15 October 2012. See also Michael Dobbs, *One Minute to Midnight: Kennedy, Khrushchev, and Castro on the Brink of Nuclear War* (New York: Alfred A. Knopf, 2009); Sheldon M. Stern, *The Cuban Missile Crisis in American Memory: Myths Versus Reality* (Palo Alto, CA: Stanford University Press, 2012); and Serhii

Plokhy, 'The Real Lessons of the Cuban Missile Crisis', *Wall Street Journal*, 9 April 2021.

18 Glenn Kessler, 'An "Eyeball to Eyeball" Moment that Never Happened', *Washington Post*, 23 June 2014.

Book Reviews

Russia and Eurasia
Angela Stent

The Story of Russia
Orlando Figes. London: Bloomsbury Publishing, 2022.
£25.00. 348 pp.

Russia's invasion of Ukraine has highlighted the battle between two historical narratives about Kievan Rus' and the origins of the Russian and Ukrainian states. Vladimir Putin claims that the Russian state was born in Kyiv and that there is no separate Ukrainian nationhood. Ukrainians vigorously deny this. In this informative recounting of Russia's complex history, Figes explains that it is 'absurd' to claim that Kievan Rus' was the origin of either country. Instead, this debate illustrates Figes's observation that 'Russia is a country held together by ideas rooted in its distant past, histories continuously reconfigured and repurposed to suit its present needs and reimagine its future' (p. 6). He analyses how Russia's changing historical narratives have shaped the current Putin system.

By the eighteenth century, according to the author, Russia had evolved as a patrimonial, personal autocracy, unlike the other European absolutist states. The concept of the state and the tsar were fused in the person of a single, divinely ordained monarch. The state as a separate entity did not exist. Figes explores the debates between later generations of Russian historians about the legacy of the Mongol conquest of Russia. Should one blame the Mongol 'yoke' for Russia's enduring autocracy and failure to become part of the European family? Figes believes that the persistence of autocracy in Russia is explained less by the strength of the state than by the weakness of society, a perpetual feature of Russian history.

Despite the Europeanness of classical Russian culture, Russians have always been ambivalent about their ties to the West, and have at best been reluctant

Survival | vol. 65 no. 1 | February–March 2023 | pp. 155–161   https://doi.org/10.1080/00396338.2023.2172864

Europeans. Figes traces the origins of Russian anti-Westernism to the eighteenth century, to a national narrative based on the defence of Russian customs and morals against the corrupting influence of the West – a familiar theme in Putin's Russia. Russia's subsequent defeat in the Crimean War exacerbated feelings of humiliation by and resentment toward the West. The modern-day Kremlin's incessant talk of 'Russophobia' and Western 'hypocrisy' has deep historical roots.

The cult of the Second World War has become a cornerstone of Putin's tenure, including his likening of Ukraine to Nazi Germany. Figes explains why the USSR was able to prevail over Germany: 'The cult of sacrifice was a more important factor than terror. It was the Soviet system's main advantage over Western liberal societies where the loss of human life was given greater weight in the reckoning of the command' (p. 240).

In discussing the failure of democracy to take root in Russia after 1991, Figes reminds his readers that what is called the Putin system began during the Yeltsin years. The KGB reappeared under a new name, and old elites returned to power. Putin has reasserted Russia's 'traditional values' – patriotism, collectivism and submission to the state. There has been no reckoning with the Stalinist past. Russia is a fallen empire taking revenge on its former colony, Ukraine. The Russia that emerges from this war 'will be poorer, more unpredictable and more isolated from the world' (p. 301).

Dark Shadows: Inside the Secret World of Kazakhstan
Joanna Lillis. London: Bloomsbury Academic, 2022. £12.99.
352 pp.

The year 2022 was a turbulent one for Kazakhstan. Riots in January led to the sidelining of the Nazarbayev family, which had ruled the country for three decades. Russia sent troops to assist President Qasym-Jomurt Toqaev in quelling the unrest weeks before Vladimir Putin launched his war on Ukraine. Toqaev was quick to distance himself from that conflict, however, refusing to recognise Russia's subsequent annexation of four Ukrainian territories. After holding snap elections that he handily won, he has focused on manoeuvring between Russia, China and the West, while trying to maintain stability in a multi-ethnic country with enormous disparities in wealth and living standards.

Joanna Lillis, a British journalist living in Kazakhstan, offers an insightful explanation of how the country works in this updated version of *Dark Shadows*, completed just after the January unrest. She describes the evolution of Nursultan Nazarbayev's patronal state as he eliminated any meaningful opposition to his rule, while his family and friends enriched themselves. Oil played a key role: the author describes it as both a blessing and a curse. When prices were high,

Nazarbayev's social contract with the people – they acquiesced to his authoritarian rule while he delivered rising living standards – worked. But as petrodollars dried up, the pact began to fall apart. Labour unrest with deadly consequences in the oilfields of Zhanaozen in 2011 and again in 2022 revealed long-standing grievances about low wages, unemployment and corrupt officials.

A key challenge for Kazakhstan has been forging a viable national identity in a country where ethnic Kazakhs formed a minority of the population in 1991. In 2014, Putin offered Nazarbayev a barbed compliment when he praised him for his leadership because 'the Kazakhs never had statehood' (p. 127). Nazarbayev soon organised an extravagant celebration of the 550th anniversary of Kazakhstan's statehood in 2015, commemorating the first khanate from 1465. Kazakhstan's search for a national narrative has been aided by Russia's invasion of Ukraine, which has caused Kazakhs to confront Russia's colonial occupation of Kazakh lands. Lillis talks to Russian Cossacks who inhabit northern Kazakhstan and reminds readers that Alexander Solzhenitsyn advocated for a Slavic Union composed of Russia, Belarus, Ukraine and Northern Kazakhstan – sentiments echoed today in the Kremlin.

Toqaev promised his people that he would be in 'listening mode' when he came to power in 2019, and that he would open up society. But so far the pace of change has been glacial. The origins of the unrest in January remain obscure, with Toqaev laying the blame on foreign and domestic terrorists who were trying to topple him. He used this explanation to oust Nazarbayev from his position as Security Council chairman and arrested and subsequently put on trial Nazarbayev's security chief, Karim Masimov, on treason charges. In the aftermath of these dramatic events, Toqaev has continued to pursue a respectful, but more distanced, relationship with Russia, intensifying ties with China and pursuing greater outreach to Europe and the United States.

The Fight of Our Lives: My Time with Zelenskyy, Ukraine's Battle for Democracy, and What It Means for the World
Iuliia Mendel. New York: One Signal Publishers, 2022.
$27.99. 240 pp.

Volodymyr Zelenskyy has rightfully been praised for his courage and leadership, which have inspired Ukrainians to fight the Russian invaders so effectively since the war began in February 2022. But one should not forget that the timing of the invasion was inspired in part by the disarray then present in Ukrainian domestic politics, Zelenskyy's low popularity compared with the early days of his presidency in 2019, and Vladimir Putin's belief that there would be little resistance to the Russian army.

In her memoir, Iuliia Mendel, who served as Zelenskyy's press secretary from 2019 to 2021, paints a vivid picture of the fractious and corrupt politics in Ukraine prior to the outbreak of the war; of Zelenskyy's attempts to reform the system; and of the challenges to his leadership from his predecessor, Petro Poroshenko, and other opposition politicians. Mendel grew up in Kherson and describes how corruption in the education system almost deprived her of her PhD because she refused to pay a bribe to her supervisor. She became a journalist and was hired by Zelenskyy, who had won 73% of the popular vote. Prior to that, he had been a successful comedian and businessman, but had no political experience. The majority of those elected to the Rada from Zelenskyy's political party, Servant of the People, were also political novices.

Zelenskyy ran on a peace platform, promising to end the war in the Donbas region that had been ongoing since 2014, when Russian proxies initiated it. At issue was the Minsk II agreement, signed in 2015 when Ukraine was in a weak military position. Neither Russia nor Ukraine had implemented their part of the agreement, because they disagreed on the sequencing of its provisions. In December 2019, Zelenskyy had his first – and only – meeting with Putin in Paris under the auspices of the 'Normandy Format'. Mendel contrasts Zelenskyy's direct and persuasive negotiating style with that of Putin: 'He kept repeating himself, stammering and pausing, spitting out that Russia was not a participant in the military conflict in the Donbas, although everyone at the table knew that was not true' (p. 95). Her conclusion: 'Putin knew how to give orders, but he didn't know how to negotiate' (p. 96). After Russia launched its invasion, the Minsk II agreement was effectively dead.

Mendel discusses the outsize role of the oligarchs in the Ukrainian system. They own political parties, television stations and other media, have their own political agendas and have resisted anti-corruption reforms because these threaten their interests. She blames them for impeding Zelenskyy's reform efforts prior to the war. She further argues that the most powerful oligarchs also played a significant – and often negative – role in shaping Ukraine's international image. Once the war broke out, the oligarchs mainly rallied behind their president. But, Mendel warns, removing the oligarchs' influence on Ukrainian politics will remain a major challenge once the war is over.

The Russia Conundrum: How the West Fell for Putin's Power Gambit – And How to Fix It
Mikhail Khodorkovsky with Martin Sixsmith. New York: St. Martin's Press, 2022. $29.99. 352 pp.

Mikhail Khodorkovsky, once Russia's richest man as head of Yukos, its largest oil company, spent ten years in his country's harsh prison system because he challenged Vladimir Putin and because Igor Sechin, a Putin ally, coveted Yukos, which he subsequently took over. Now living in London and supporting Russians who oppose Putin and the war in Ukraine, Khodorkovsky has written a memoir dissecting the Putin system and setting forth an agenda for positive change after Putin is no longer in the Kremlin.

Raised in a rough Moscow neighbourhood, he rose in the ranks of the Komsomol (Young Communist League), and when Mikhail Gorbachev permitted private business, he and fellow students set up Menatep, a computer company. After the Soviet collapse, it became a major private bank, and Khodorkovsky became one of the wealthiest new oligarchs. In 1996, he joined with fellow magnates to provide financial support to Boris Yeltsin during his difficult re-election campaign. In return, Khodorkovsky was able to purchase Yukos on very favourable terms, 'a turning point for me that would define the rest of my life' (p. 49).

After his 2003 arrest and trial, Khodorkovsky was sent to a harsh labour camp in Siberia, where he was frequently thrown into punishment cells and was stabbed by another inmate. Nevertheless, he says the brutal camp regime was preferable to prison: 'in prison you are locked in a small room with the same people all day; in the camp you can walk around as much as you want. The sun, the sky, greenery in the summer, which in prison you can't see, is all important for a person's wellbeing' (p. 163).

Khodorkovsky writes that when Putin was deputy mayor of St Petersburg, he co-opted organised-crime bosses to minimise outbreaks of violence, and in return everyone received a share of profits from various extortion rackets. Once he became president, the former KGB case officer elevated the FSB to become the system's favoured elite. Khodorkovsky draws a straight line from Putin's St Petersburg days to the development of what he calls a 'mafia state' in Russia, in which the security services are entwined with organised crime. Putin, along with a few thousand people working for the Kremlin, constitutes the core of this state and controls most of the nation's wealth.

But wealth alone does not motivate Putin, argues Khodorkovsky. The Russian president bears deep grievances against the West, and in his rewriting of history 'wishes to create a narrative of continuity between the eras of tsarism, communism and the present day, in which Russia appears as an imperial power, equaling and rivaling the West, exerting strength and influence across the globe' (p. 237).

Despite his pessimism about Russia's current political system, Khodorkovsky insists that he is optimistic about the future. He believes that Putin will be the last Russian autocrat and that a new generation of Russians who value freedom, the rule of law and democracy will emerge to create a different Russia.

Putin's Trolls: On the Frontlines of Russia's Information War Against the World
Jessikka Aro. New York: Ig Publishing, 2022. $18.95. 375 pp.

Jessikka Aro is an investigative journalist specialising in Russian information warfare via social media. She was forced to leave her homeland after the emergence of libellous news articles and threats to her life from Russian information warriors and their supporters in the West. Her book combines harrowing personal experiences with some of the most notorious cases of Russian information warfare, presenting a sobering picture of how effective Russia has been in spreading conspiracy theories and relativising the truth.

Ukraine has been a particular target. In 2016, the Ukrainian Cyber Alliance hacked into an email account of Vladislav Surkov, an adviser to Vladimir Putin. These emails showed that Putin's inner circle had played a key role in engineering the conflict in the Donbas and the Russian invasion in 2014. They also contained detailed instructions for specific media operations in the Donbas region. Russia counter-attacked, claiming that Surkov did not use email. That campaign was organised by Alexander Dugin, the ultra-nationalist who supported the creation of a new state, 'Novorossiya', in the Donbas region. Russia has further escalated its information warfare in Ukraine since the 2022 invasion.

Aro documents how Russia targets far-right and neo-Nazi groups in Scandinavia to amplify its campaigns. These groups, she writes, admire Putin as 'a master judoka, muscular fisherman, fighter jet pilot and of course, war mastermind who enforces "healthy nationalism"' (p. 172). Their admiration for Putin is driven by anti-Americanism, anti-globalism and their view of Russia as the last bastion of 'traditional values'.

Russia has increasingly targeted Serbians who advocate for a pro-Western, democratic Serbia in the European Union and NATO. Russian information warriors have issued death threats to pro-Western Serbian activists, and have successfully manipulated social media to cast doubt in the minds of many Serbians about the wisdom of integration with Europe.

One of the most notorious Russian disinformation campaigns has been Moscow's refusal to accept responsibility for the downing in 2014 of MH17, the Malaysian airliner flying from Amsterdam over Ukraine to Kuala Lumpur. All 298 people on board perished. The principal target of this campaign has been Eliot Higgins, a British investigative journalist and founder of the open-source website Bellingcat, which first revealed the truth – that MH17 was shot down by a Russian *Buk* missile. Over the years, the Kremlin has pushed a variety of conspiracy theories to explain the crash, none of which involve Russia. After the crash, a new pro-Kremlin fake-news website called Russia Insider was created.

Claiming to be crowdsourced, it describes what it sees as the United States' 'degeneracy' and has a special section demonising Jews. It has focused much of its ire on Higgins, depicting him as a US lackey and an idiot. In 2018, Putin denied, from the stage of the St. Petersburg International Economic Forum, that a Russian missile had destroyed MH17. In this case, however, the Kremlin did not prevail. An Amsterdam court tried and convicted *in absentia* two Russians and a Ukrainian proxy responsible for the downing of the flight.

Africa
Karen Smith

Against Decolonisation: Taking African Agency Seriously
Olúfẹ́mi Táíwò. London: C. Hurst & Co., 2022. £14.99. 270 pp.

This is a courageous book with a controversial title that is bound to elicit debate. Olúfẹ́mi Táíwò makes the case that the indiscriminate application of the term 'decolonisation' to a range of issues has resulted in the continued denial of agency to Africans, and an impoverishment of scholarship on the continent. His main criticism is what he calls the 'absolutisation of colonialism' (p. 7), which entails viewing colonialism as the defining event in African history, and a problematic conflation between modernity and colonialism. He contends that the latter in particular leads to the flawed argument that liberation from colonialism requires a rejection of all the trappings of modernity.

One of his main concerns is that, because of an 'obsession with decolonisation' (p. 139), much of the rich heritage of African intellectual work is being overlooked. He claims that work by Africans who have either developed similar ideas, or chosen to adopt or adapt Western ideas, is dismissed out of hand, thereby denying them agency. Táíwò cautions against the uncritical romanticisation of anything 'indigenous' and the wholesale rejection of anything with a whiff of the West. By drawing on examples of the work of African thinkers and writers, he aims to showcase ways in which they have domesticated ideas and practices that have their roots in modernity, and calls on scholars – especially young African scholars – to engage with the intellectual legacy of African scholarship in its totality.

While Táíwò's arguments are well founded, it is important not to diminish the destructive impact of colonialism on African societies, including on the production of knowledge and culture. At times, the author ascribes too much agency to individuals and neglects the structural constraints imposed by Western hegemony and spread via the colonial project. For example, he notes that writers from former colonies are free to write in the language of their choice, but if we consider that education systems were and continue to be shaped by colonial practices (including language choices), and that, partly through colonialism, English has become the lingua franca for academic scholarship aimed at a global audience, this becomes a difficult argument to make. Similarly, when he asks why we need to decolonise a field like philosophy instead of simply recognising that philosophy (or for that matter international relations) would be richer if it included views from around the world, he is choosing to ignore

Survival | vol. 65 no. 1 | February–March 2023 | pp. 162–168   https://doi.org/10.1080/00396338.2023.2172865

the ways in which Western-centrism has had disciplining and gatekeeping effects on the academy as a whole. His argument also relies on generalisations about scholars engaging in decolonisation discourse, assuming, for example, that their shared aim is a return to a pre-colonial condition. He demands that use of the term 'decolonisation' be limited to the original meaning of political self-determination, contending that 'you cannot decolonise in a situation where "the colonial world" is no more' (p. 25). In this sense, he appears to be missing the point that post-colonial thinkers are making – that colonialism did not end with the political independence of former colonies – although Táíwò also cautions against equating neo-colonialism with colonialism. Another limitation of *Against Decolonisation* is that the writing is quite repetitive, clearly a product of the author's determination to forcefully make his case.

Despite these shortcomings, Táíwò's contention that knowledge is always the result of a combination of influences, making it difficult to clearly distinguish between what is colonial, Western or authentically African, is a relevant one in an era in which societies in all parts of the world are grappling with Western-centrism and colonial legacies. There is clearly much work left to be done, and this book makes an original and timely contribution to these efforts.

Africa's Struggle for Its Art: History of a Postcolonial Defeat
Bénédicte Savoy. Princeton, NJ: Princeton University Press,
2022. £25.00/$29.95. 214 pp.

The numbers speak for themselves: the Royal Museum for Central Africa in Tervuren, Belgium, holds 180,000 objects from Africa; the British Museum, 69,000 (p. vi). The debate about the restitution of cultural artefacts held by former colonial powers such as Belgium, France, Germany, the Netherlands and the United Kingdom has been given new impetus by a renewed societal awareness of the continuing legacy of colonialism in the form of systemic racism and seemingly intractable historical inequalities between European states and former colonies.

Africa's Struggle for Its Art, a highly readable and meticulously researched overview of the cultural-restitution debate in Europe, comes to us from Bénédicte Savoy, a historian and co-author of the report 'The Restitution of African Cultural Heritage' (the 'Sarr–Savoy Report'), which was commissioned by French President Emmanuel Macron in 2017. In a history that begins in the 1960s, this volume challenges the narrative that this is a recent discussion, even if much of it has largely been forgotten. Drawing on an impressive range of archival material, Savoy provides a year-by-year account of major milestones, including Mobutu Sese Seko's address to the United Nations General Assembly in 1973 and the establishment of an intergovernmental restitution committee by UNESCO in 1978. The author also explores the role of museums, the media and key individuals on both sides of the debate. It is clearly important to her to emphasise the understudied role of women, and she mentions a handful of examples, claiming that 'it was often women in Europe who showed solidarity with the claimant African countries' (p. 2).

While the focus is on Germany within the wider European context, the book also details the first calls for restitution from newly independent African states in the 1960s. At the heart of the book is Savoy's attempt to solve the puzzle of how and by whom calls for restitution were so effectively silenced during this time. The author investigates specific strategies employed by European museums and administrations to deliberately evade restitution claims and systematically prevent the return of colonial-period holdings, including the deliberate withholding of inventories in the case of the Federal Republic of Germany. The records she uncovers show the origins of now well-rehearsed but mostly baseless arguments against restitution, including that of cultural guardianship and the idea of cultural universalism. These tactics often brought museums in conflict with foreign ministries, who regarded the question of cultural restitution as one that could influence sensitive relationships with newly independent states. Savoy mentions, for example, how the British Foreign and Commonwealth Office unsuccessfully put pressure on the British Museum to grant loans of artworks to Nigeria.

International-relations scholars have increasingly realised that the discipline has not paid enough attention to culture, including its importance in understanding the behaviour of and relations between states. This is a fascinating and highly recommended read for anyone interested in an often overlooked dynamic that continues to influence North–South relations.

The Country That Does Not Exist: A History of Somaliland
Gérard Prunier. London: C. Hurst & Company, 2021. £45.00.
279 pp.

Gérard Prunier considers why Somaliland – a stable, peaceful and democratic country that meets all the criteria of successful statehood – is still not recognised by the international community, while Somalia, its 'failed state' neighbour, is. In response to the critique that 'the past is often neglected by contemporary researchers' (p. 80), the author takes the reader on a historical tour through the painful birth of a country whose existence the world refuses to acknowledge. Employing an interdisciplinary approach that draws on history as well as anthropology, his research goes beyond superficial or abstract theoretical assumptions in a bid to understand the connections between geography, social structures and the challenges faced by Somalis in meeting the demands of the post-colonial world order.

Prunier takes a critical approach to the existing Westphalian state system and its accompanying Eurocentric legal order, questioning the assumption of its universal applicability to a people like the Somali, for whom he claims 'the state was not only something irrelevant, it was an annoyance and, at worst, an instrument for obstruction and oppression' (p. 3). He provides a comprehensive examination of the incompatibility – complicated by the region's colonial history – of the Somali clan system with statehood, and a dense and detailed account of the origins and development of the civil war in the 1980s. The role played by external actors in the context of the Cold War is also showcased, with the author especially critical of the initial complacency – and in the case of the United States, culpability – of the international community in the face of large-scale killings, as well as the ignorance and arrogance of the eventual intervention. The ironic importance of the Somali diaspora, particularly in the United Kingdom, in fostering a sense of nationalism and contributing to the creation of the Somali National Movement (SNM) is perceptively highlighted. The text is interspersed with long excerpts from interviews with SNM members, including eyewitness accounts of the brutal violence committed by the different sides. It is a convoluted story, and it can be difficult to keep track of the various actors, geographical areas and events. The drawback of an exhaustive historical account is that the reader can get caught up in the detail, losing sight of more general dynamics.

Only in the last two chapters (10 and 11) does the author return to the original question of the lack of recognition for Somaliland, but he does not engage with the multiple legal and political explanations. Critical of international attempts at 'rebuilding' something (the Somali state) that had never really existed in the first place, the author provides an implicit critique of the post-Second World War liberal order and the liberal-peacebuilding efforts of the United Nations and the wider international community. As an alternative, he commends the success of local, traditional peacebuilding efforts.

Significantly, Prunier provides an insightful explanation of how the Somali experience was radically different from decolonisation movements in other African countries. For the latter, the challenge was creating a sense of nationhood to support the inherited colonial state, while for the Somali, the challenge was that their nation had been split across five states. As a result, while most African nation-states opted to maintain existing colonial borders, the Somali wanted to dismantle them, something the author claims was regarded as a major threat by the international powers that be. Ultimately, 'the collapse of the "united" Somali state opened a legal gap in the post-colonial logic, a situation where reality and legality no longer coincided' (p. 201). The book elicits reflection on the unquestioning belief in and commitment to the pre-eminence of the Westphalian state system.

Understanding South Africa
Carien du Plessis and Martin Plaut. London: C. Hurst &
Company, 2019. £22.00. 316 pp.

What happened to Desmond Tutu's 'rainbow nation', which was meant to emerge from South Africa's transition to full democracy under the leadership of Nelson Mandela? Almost 30 years after the end of apartheid, two seasoned journalists investigate the current state of affairs in a highly divided South Africa. They provide a critical analysis of the complex and interdependent historical, socio-political and economic factors that have contributed to shattering the dreams of millions of South Africans.

While the emphasis is on contemporary challenges, with chapters on topics such as corruption and education, the book begins with a brief overview of the country's history intended to familiarise readers with South Africa's political landscape. The historically informed account includes summaries of the main news stories and scandals of the past 30 years, tracing contemporary societal ills to the apartheid era and earlier. For example, the complicity of the five permanent members of the United Nations Security Council and of global banks in assisting South Africa's state-owned companies to contravene the 1977 arms embargo is cited as an example of corruption dating back to the National Party administration, mirroring the arms-deal scandal under the Mbeki administration. The authors succeed in treading a fine line in criticising the African National Congress (ANC)-led government for its failures while also acknowledging how the challenges South Africa faces today are deeply connected to its troubled past, with appropriate blame being apportioned to the legacy of apartheid-era policies.

The book ends with a chapter on President Cyril Ramaphosa who, despite having been accused of serious misconduct, was recently re-elected as leader of the ANC. Discussion of his presidency in *Understanding South Africa* ends with the 2019 election, and only briefly touches on his early failures to tackle the scourge of corruption, which by now could constitute another volume. This problem, together with high levels of crime and unemployment, and seemingly intractable infrastructure problems, has entrenched a sense of disillusionment that has been growing over the past decade.

An easy read, this book offers a succinct overview of the intricacies of South Africa's complex society, from the ideological struggles within the ruling party to the involvement of three Indian brothers in what came to be seen as state capture during the Zuma administration. Despite the challenges it faces, South Africa remains an important player on the African continent, its fate closely tied to that of its neighbours. *Understanding South Africa* is therefore essential reading for anyone hoping to make sense not only of the country, but also of the wider region.

African Political Thought: An Intellectual History of the Quest for Freedom
Stephen Chan. London: C. Hurst & Co., 2021. £18.99. 262 pp.

Due to the cultural hegemony of the West, few international-relations scholars or political scientists will be familiar with African political thinkers beyond Nelson Mandela. Stephen Chan seeks to overcome this ignorance in *African Political Thought*, finding in the speeches and writings of African leaders an often overlooked resource.

Offering a condensed who's who of leading figures in African independence struggles, interspersed with thinkers such as Frantz Fanon and Achille Mbembe, Chan's focus is more on the context in which they developed their thoughts than on any in-depth engagement with their ideas. The author's observation in a chapter on Robert Mugabe that 'I have developed my comments on, if not his political thought, then the context of his thought' (p. 123) applies equally to the other figures reviewed. That said, Chan does not shy away from pointing out the contradictions and fallacies in their ideas, noting, for instance, that some innovative and emancipatory philosophies about governance were often coercively enforced through one-party states.

One question that is largely sidestepped is that of what constitutes African political thought, including debates about the extent to which culture influences knowledge. Similarly, Africans' unique contributions to global political thought are not afforded sufficient prominence. While brief mention is made of the fact that the African Union's concept of 'non-indifference' – which replaced the Organisation of African Unity's commitment to non-intervention – can be regarded as a forerunner to the 'responsibility to protect' (p. 168), and that Amícal Cabral proposed an alternative understanding of class formation that was not dependent on the European industrial model, neither is discussed explicitly as having made an innovative contribution to global political thought.

Ultimately, the book reads like an extended conversation with Chan about Africa's twentieth-century history and some of the individuals whose thinking shaped the continent's trajectory during this time, interspersed with personal snippets about the author's experiences living in and visiting various countries.

As in any conversation, there are frequent jumps in the narrative – a paragraph about Kenneth Kaunda and Cabral suddenly shifts to a discussion of the Cuban Missile Crisis, and in a section on the Black Panthers, the author shares an anecdote about how Hugh Masekela got his first trumpet. But the connections Chan draws between seemingly unrelated people and events is also precisely what makes for stimulating reading. For readers interested in an accessible overview of a selected cast of characters who played a significant role in Africa's independence struggles and post-independence development, this is a worthwhile read, but scholars expecting an in-depth engagement with specific strands of thought will be left disappointed.

Asia-Pacific
Lanxin Xiang

Subimperial Power: Australia in the International Arena
Clinton Fernandes. Melbourne: Melbourne University Press,
2022. A$24.99. 176 pp.

Clinton Fernandes examines the long-established claim that Australia is a 'middle power' trying to uphold a 'rules-based international order'. Rejecting these terms as euphemisms, he argues that Australia is merely a subimperial power upholding a US-led imperial order. An empire, notes Fernandes, is 'a relationship, formal or informal, in which one state controls the effective political sovereignty of others' (p. 10). 'Being an imperial power', he continues, 'means exerting a controlling influence on other countries' sovereignty. Control can be achieved without conquering colonies or directly ruling foreign lands … Today the United States sits at the apex of a hierarchically structured imperial system' (p. 10).

A subimperial power is not a victim but a beneficiary, and hence a junior partner within the system. The author argues that Australia has long been a subimperial power, first under British rule and now within an American-led empire. This does not make it an exploited neo-colony of the US, but an active player in an imperial system – the so-called 'rules-based international order' – that it is working to uphold, because doing so best serves its national interests.

Fernandes takes issue with the very idea of a rules-based international order. Such an order 'is not an inclusive order created for the benefit of humanity', he writes. 'It does not mean a peaceful and harmonious system, despite its benign-sounding name.' Instead, he makes the case that 'international orders are power politics by procedural means. They entrench the power of powerful states and help them exclude and subdue their rivals' (p. 4). He argues that the major international orders of the past four centuries, all dominated by white Europeans, were 'orders of exclusion', designed by dominant powers to 'ostracise and outcompete rivals'. Examples include the Treaty of Westphalia, designed to undermine the authority of the Catholic Church and the Holy Roman Empire; the post-Napoleonic peace established in Vienna to allow conservative monarchies to counter the rise of liberal revolutionary regimes; and the order we live under today, defined by 'the primacy of the first hegemonic actor in history to be a full liberal democracy, the United States of America' (p. 4).

Imperial power centres always demand military inter-operability, says Fernandes, hence AUKUS is nothing new. Even before the First World War, Australia was concerned with the inter-operability of its forces with those of

Britain, the leading imperial power at the time (p. 8). The AUKUS project will allow Australia to uphold its subimperial 'way of war', which has long been 'to operate inside the strategy of a superpower by contributing a niche capability to augment the larger force' (p. 5).

Has the rules-based international order served to promote world peace? Not at all, according to the author, who notes that, during the Cold War, the US tried to 'change other nations' governments' 72 times, with 66 covert operations and six overt ones. 'It did not target a single monarchy in this period; 28 per cent of covert operations targeted democracies' (p. 15). Today, the rules-based international order is 'not intended to limit US–China competition … The writing of exclusionary rules is part of the competition, not a way to avoid it' (p. 5). This is an outstanding critical history.

Winning by Process: The State and Neutralization of Ethnic Minorities in Myanmar
Jacques Bertrand, Alexandre Pelletier and Ardeth Maung Thawnghmung. Ithaca, NY: Cornell University Press, 2022. $29.95. 270 pp.

In February 2021, the armed forces of Myanmar (the Tatmadaw) detained Aung San Suu Kyi and other high-ranking politicians after a contested election with disputed results. The coup has been widely criticised abroad as a return to pre-2011 Myanmar politics characterised by widespread civil conflict and human-rights abuses.

The authors of *Winning by Process* examine a decade of apparently missed opportunities from a different angle, analysing the peace process in Myanmar between 2011 and 2021. Asking 'why progress toward a peace agreement remained elusive, despite all parties suffering from war fatigue and wanting civil war to end', they argue that 'while the 2021 coup might suggest that the previous decade [of civilian rule] was merely a sham, we disagree with such an interpretation' (p. 2). Through detailed study, they find that the Tatmadaw decided to allow a democratic process to start in 2011 precisely because its previous 'divide-and-rule' strategies for dealing with minority rebels had failed. 'After 2011, it launched a decade of attempted negotiations as part of its so-called "road map to democracy," not only to reintroduce a form of civilian government but also to end the civil war' (p. 2).

The authors label this approach 'winning by process' and contrast it with its two 'well-known and well-theorized alternatives', winning by war and winning by agreement. In winning by war, one of the sides defeats its opponent, 'either by crushing it or taking over the state' (p. 11). In winning by agreement, a negotiated peace settlement is reached that generally reconfigures state institutions by establishing guaranteed representation, legislative vetoes, power sharing or territorial autonomy. The authors wish to draw attention to 'how process produces and shapes a whole set of outcomes that fall in between' victory by war or agreement. 'Commonly referred to as "stalemates" or "protracted conflicts"', they write, 'these outcomes are often ignored as transient points on a trajectory toward peace or losing in war' (p. 11).

After Aung San Suu Kyi and her National League for Democracy (NLD) came to power in a landslide election victory in 2015, they were expected to

> push forward reforms and [forge] a new relationship with ethnic minority groups. Yet it became quickly apparent that they failed … to make any significant progress on peace negotiations or on restructuring the governance of ethnic minority states toward their goal of federalism. Instead, Aung San Suu Kyi sought to recentralize the state … The NLD also relied heavily on strong support from the Bamar majority, which was mainly lukewarm on the idea of federalism and greater concessions toward ethnic minority groups. (p. 73)

The Tatmadaw staged its coup to regain control over civilian rule but did not intend to bring about the end of the peace process (p. 4). This process may have appeared stalled, but it had allowed the state to centralise its power and to contain violence 'without much compromise or costly war' (p. 3). In other words, the state was 'winning by process'. Unfortunately for the Tatmadaw, its interference has served to reverse many of the state's gains by triggering a 'downward spiral of violence' (p. 2).

The Making of the Modern Philippines: Pieces of a Jigsaw State
Philip Bowring. London: Bloomsbury Academic, 2022.
£20.00. 272 pp.

The Philippines stands out among its Southeast Asian neighbours for several reasons. Its name has been in use for more than 500 years, longer than those of most regional states, although it was historically dominated by Western powers, first Spain and then the United States. It is the only predominantly Catholic nation in the region, even though it is culturally affiliated with the Malay Peninsula, where Muslim culture dominates. Its 'island chain separating the Pacific Ocean from the South China Sea, and hence the Indian Ocean, is strategically vital to bigger powers' (p. 4). It has close ties to the United States, but also cultivates a good relationship with China, America's twenty-first-century nemesis.

Philip Bowring believes that the country's lack of a national language and weak sense of national identity have hampered the state in exerting effective governance. Constitutionally speaking, the Philippines is a unitary state, but it does not have a centralised civil service. Decisions made in 'imperial Manila' are bound to be implemented poorly in the provinces, which tend to manage their own affairs. The country's economic performance lags behind that of most of its neighbours, because the government offers few incentives to investment, domestic or international. Widespread corruption and tariff walls further limit development. In foreign policy, the country cannot fully embrace the United States' 'Indo-Pacific Strategy' because of its close economic ties with China. The US and other littoral states were 'stunned' when president Rodrigo Duterte set aside the Philippines' 2016 court victory over China at the Permanent Court of Arbitration in The Hague, a case Manila had brought in response to Chinese claims and activities in the South China Sea (pp. 95, 235).

The author laments that 'the need for change is self-evident, but how to get there is not' (p. 234). The idea of establishing a federal state is unlikely to take root, given that Filipinos cannot even decide which regions should be considered the founding parts of a federal system. What the Philippines urgently needs, says Bowring, is a 'revolution to throw off the old elites, end monopolies, open up to foreign competition, prioritize education, eliminate large-scale smuggling and enforce taxes' (p. 234). The author concludes that 'the nation, like its archipelago, is made up of many odd-shaped pieces' that are bound together by a 500-year history that in some cases has bequeathed institutions long in need of change. It is a country with untapped potential awaiting a 'shake-up which would enable its people's talents [to] be better reflected in the state of the nation' (p. 237).

Taiwan, the United States, and the Hidden History of the Cold War in Asia: Divided Allies
Hsiao-Ting Lin. Abingdon: Routledge, 2022. £120.00. 260 pp.

How has American policy toward Taiwan been formulated, and how has it changed over time? It is easy to assume that the cooperation between the Americans and the Chinese Nationalists after 1949 was similar to the alliances Washington established with 'other anti-communist entities in Asia' during the Cold War. However, Hsiao-Ting Lin finds that

> the relationship was often characterized by a considerable degree
> of mutual distrust and was hampered by a blend of nationalism,
> pragmatism, and opportunism on the part of the Chinese Nationalists. It

was also often overshadowed by the political calculations on both sides of the alliance and their respective leaders' intentions to maximize their own national interests. (p. 3)

There is an irony surrounding US Taiwan policy. On the one hand, Washington has clearly favoured a 'politically stable, pro-American regime on Taiwan, although it was unwilling to commit many resources to this goal until the outbreak of the Korean War'. On the other hand, Taiwan was a dictatorship for most of the Cold War period. One might have expected this to sit uneasily with the United States' purported commitment to freedom and democracy, but the island's political stability and military strength were seen as more important than any social or political reforms that might have undermined the military or destabilised national institutions.

Still, ideological differences between Washington and Taipei produced a relationship that the author characterises as 'divided allies'. Indeed, American ambivalence toward Taiwan resulted in numerous meetings between the government of Chiang Kai-shek and Mao Zedong – during the offshore-island crisis in the 1950s, for example – that would ultimately help to reduce the tension between the US and the People's Republic of China. In chapter 3, Lin describes how 'U.S. policy chiefs were both annoyed and bewildered' when Chiang refused to support the Dalai Lama's cause during the 1959 Tibetan uprising. 'A huge anticommunist crisis that supposedly should have united the Free World instead essentially pushed Taipei closer to Beijing and the Communist bloc', he writes (p. 94). The fact that Chiang was a fervent nationalist and Han Chinese irredentist certainly played a decisive role in his handling of Tibet.

Today, 'Taiwan is seen by many Americans as an important ally in their Indo-Pacific strategy' and a partner in containing the People's Republic (p. 212). Lin offers a nuanced picture of a complex relationship that may be further developed as archival materials from the post-Cold War era are declassified.

Closing Argument

The Weakness of Indispensable Leaders

Erik Jones

I

It took four days and 15 ballots for Kevin McCarthy, the US House of Representatives' Republican leader, to win enough votes to become speaker of the House. Even the first failed ballot had started whispers that McCarthy should withdraw from the contest in the interest of Congress and the American people. If he could not lead his own Republican Conference, how could he hope to lead the House of Representatives? But McCarthy persevered, cajoling and kowtowing his way to the gavel he had long coveted and felt entitled to wield. McCarthy's critics among Democratic politicians and the media said he had weakened his position through concessions to the militant cadre of MAGA Republicans. His Republican supporters insisted that McCarthy had earned the right to be speaker.[1]

If there was an important point of agreement in the election of the new speaker, it was that nobody claimed that McCarthy was indispensable. On the contrary, everyone admitted that there were others who could lead the Republican Conference if necessary. They acknowledged that McCarthy was ambitious, that he had long aspired to the position, that he still bore deep scars over not receiving the post in 2015 – when outgoing speaker John Boehner anointed Paul Ryan instead – and that he would go to great lengths to achieve his personal goal. Some observers feared that McCarthy's ambitions were exacting too high a price from the House and

Erik Jones is director of the Robert Schuman Centre for Advanced Studies at the European University Institute.

Survival | vol. 65 no. 1 | February–March 2023 | pp. 175–184   https://doi.org/10.1080/00396338.2023.2172868

176 I Erik Jones

the speakership as institutions.[2] The implication was that someone else could do the job without being forced to make the same concessions.

The circumstances of McCarthy's selection contrast sharply with those of Italy's political transition last July, when Mario Draghi, the prime minister, brought down his own government despite maintaining a majority within both chambers of the Italian parliament. Draghi was widely regarded as the country's indispensable political leader.[3] The president, Sergio Mattarella, had asked him in February 2021 to form a national-unity coalition to lead Italy out of the pandemic and undertake the painful reforms necessary to qualify for European Union assistance in rebuilding the country's economy. That coalition included virtually every major political party apart from the far-right Brothers of Italy and comprised more than 85% of the seats in parliament. Faced with a rebellion from one part of his coalition, however, Draghi reasoned that he would never be able to achieve those legislative objectives. He had no desire to hold onto power for its own sake. After a life of devoted public service, he resigned, leaving Mattarella little choice but to dissolve parliament and call for early elections.

Draghi's critics worried that his grip on his governing coalition was excessive, that he relied too heavily on confidence votes to move legislation, that he had inordinately empowered the executive branch and that the press too often gave him a free pass.[4] Muted when he was in office, those criticisms acquired greater resonance when the Brothers of Italy won the subsequent elections as the vanguard of a right-wing coalition and Giorgia Meloni replaced Draghi. Meloni, though Draghi's principal opponent, openly admires his disciplined method, strives to emulate his style of governance and aspires to strengthen the executive even further, moving it towards something like France's presidential system.[5]

Both stories are acutely relevant to understanding the resilience of political institutions, including constitutional checks and balances. McCarthy's critics claim he is weakening control over the legislature, Meloni's that she is strengthening it. Both leaders, however, face a comeuppance. If McCarthy proves unable to control the Republican Conference in the House, he will most likely be replaced as speaker, or the

Republicans will be replaced as a majority. If Meloni pushes too hard to centralise power, she too will court rebellion – particularly if she tries to bring proposed constitutional changes to the electorate via a popular referendum. But since neither leader is remotely indispensable, what matters is how good existing US and Italian constitutional arrangements are at self-correcting. The strength of democracy is precisely that political leaders are replaceable, particularly when they make mistakes. Indispensable leaders are a weakness.

II

The weakness of indispensable leaders is on full display in those countries led by strongmen sitting atop authoritarian regimes. It seems only a short time ago that these strongmen – and they are virtually all men – were heralded as a serious challenge to democracy.[6] Leaders such as Russian President Vladimir Putin, Chinese President Xi Jinping, Turkish President Recep Tayyip Erdoğan, former Brazilian president Jair Bolsonaro, Hungarian Prime Minister Viktor Orbán and Polish leader Jarosław Kaczyński offered what many saw as a refreshingly illiberal and yet still potentially attractive model of governance. So, they thought, did Donald Trump in the United States. Under that model, these leaders are irreplaceable in many respects.[7] To their supporters, they are uniquely talented and insightful. They have the special ability to act where others dither, to root out corruption, to stand up to entrenched power and to represent their people's best interests. Even their detractors concede that if any of these leaders suddenly vanished, there would be a bitter fight for power with few rules and a high potential for violence. Hence, they are seen as indispensable if only as a bulwark against chaos.

The disadvantages of this kind of political leadership are becoming more obvious. Putin is embroiled in a brutal, misguided and unnecessary conflict in Ukraine with no obvious way to extricate Russia without losing face.[8] His only alternatives are to keep pouring conscripts onto the battlefield, escalate the conflict even further or find some way to declare victory in the face of defeat. Yet a coup could trigger violent conflict within Russia. Putin is as trapped in his presidency as Russia is mired in Ukraine.[9]

Xi's position is better than Putin's – the Chinese leader has consolidated his authority over the ruling party and state institutions – but he has had similar problems in taking responsibility for his policy mistakes.[10] The recent reversal of the 'zero-COVID' policy is a good illustration. That policy was successful during the early stages of the pandemic but became more problematic as other countries relied on aggressive vaccination campaigns to open up their economies and societies. Xi could not relax the zero-COVID policy without a similarly aggressive vaccination strategy, but he also could not rely on vaccinations to strengthen immunity unless he either waited for Chinese researchers to replicate the success of Western mRNA vaccines or purchased those vaccines from the West. Both options were politically unpalatable. Pressured by mass protests and civil unrest, Xi decided simply to open up Chinese society and allow the pandemic to spread through the population.

For Erdoğan, the challenge lies in economic performance. In centralising control over the country's political institutions and economic policy, he shrank his circle of trust and invited greater political challenges both from putative allies within his party and from the opposition.[11] Now Erdoğan faces slow growth and high inflation with few viable means of improving the situation. The consequences of losing power for his family and his allies would be potentially disastrous.[12] Like Putin, he is trapped as president.

The point is not that the arrival of a strongman in office dooms any political system. On the contrary, voters in Brazil managed to push Bolsonaro out of office just as voters in the United States removed Trump. In both cases, democracy redeemed itself. It turned out that neither of these leaders was truly indispensable after all. Whether the same is true for Kaczyński – who holds no official title but leads through his Law and Justice political party – or Orbán remains to be seen. Indeed, much of the justification for the European debate about the 'rule of law' in Hungary and Poland is to ensure that their political systems remain resilient and that the two countries do not fall into the hands of irreplaceable autocrats. So long as a democratic opposition has the potential to alternate in power in both countries, it seems likely that the Hungarian and Polish political systems will eventually right themselves.[13]

III

If democratic constitutional arrangements are resilient where supposedly indispensable leaders are weak, it is fair to ask why it is important for democracies to have strong leaders and why such leaders tend to view themselves as indispensable in a way that could undermine democracy, or at least challenge fundamental democratic principles. In his recent essay 'Why American Power Endures', G. John Ikenberry argues that American power endures because the United States continues to inspire hope.[14] In turn, the US uses that power to build alliances and promote world order. 'If China and Russia seek to usher in a new world order, they will need to offer something better – an onerous task indeed.'[15]

What is striking about Ikenberry's argument is that he ascribes so little agency to US political leaders. Woodrow Wilson defined terms and made arguments, as did Franklin Delano Roosevelt, Harry Truman and George H.W. Bush, but in so doing they only described American greatness. The real political actor remained either the United States as a 'unique kind of society' or Washington as the expression of a unique political arrangement.

Ikenberry does not enlist any American presidents after George H.W. Bush in his argument for the persistence of American power, even if 'supporters of President Donald Trump' perversely deserve mention for their 'attack on the U.S. Capitol'.[16] Xi and Putin are identified as the principal challengers to American global leadership – Xi as China's 'dictator for life' and Putin by placing the United States and democracies in general 'on the defensive' through his 'gambit' in Ukraine.[17]

Ikenberry's account of American power locates agency in social movements inside and outside the United States. This reflects the conventional wisdom in the social sciences that individuals have less influence on the course of history than do the broader social movements within which they exist. This is understandable, since neither historical figures nor the historians who trace their arcs can free themselves from the context within which they operate.[18]

Ikenberry's emphasis on structural forces and large social movements also turns on the idea that most leaders are replaceable insofar as the likely alternatives would do things very similarly.[19] Even if McCarthy had stepped back after losing the first ballot for speaker of the House, his most likely replacement, Steve Scalise, would have much the same trouble managing the Republican majority in the House. In Italy, Meloni could not be more different from Draghi, and yet she is doing much the same as Draghi would have done had he remained in office.[20]

The problem with focusing so much on structures and social movements is that political power and social interests can work at cross purposes at crucial moments. Such moments call for extraordinarily enlightened leadership. Mahatma Gandhi, Václav Havel and Nelson Mandela – three 'leaders of liberation movements' whom Ikenberry highlights – were historically key to reconciling the tension between power and interests.[21] By contrast, Trump simply increased and perpetuated it by encouraging his followers to storm the US Capitol. Many of them continued to exploit that same tension as House members during McCarthy's bid to become speaker.[22]

The uneasy relationship between government and society is part and parcel of democratic life. Indeed, it is the reason democracy was created in the first place. Other forms of government are simply too rigid to adapt to a changing society, hereditary aristocracy being the most egregious. Democracy excels at ensuring the circulation of elites.[23] Unfortunately, however, that circulation is not automatic. Those who have power are reluctant to surrender it to those who do not – even in democracies. Robert Michels referred to this disposition as the 'iron law of oligarchy'.[24] By the same token, as democratic power becomes entrenched in existing elites, fresh leadership is needed to shake things up and to initiate the reforms necessary to make democratic institutions more responsive.[25]

Even more unfortunately, the way new leaders emerge in a democratic polity is uniquely unfiltered and prone to excess.[26] Part of the problem is that anyone not already part of the elite will face nearly insuperable obstacles to gaining meaningful access to the political process. The more ingrained the system becomes, the more would-be elites – Moisés Naím calls them 'aspiring autocrats' – are likely to favour disruption over accommodation.[27] Furthermore, both power and legitimacy in democracy derive from the connection between leaders and followers. The notion of charismatic leadership does not exist in aristocratic society; it is a distinctly liberal innovation.[28] And it is precisely charismatic leaders who are most inclined to regard themselves as indispensable and thus to try to position themselves as strongmen within democratic institutions.[29]

Strongmen do not offer a viable alternative to democracy. Rather, they represent the failure of democracy to adjust effectively to the rise of new social movements. The dictatorships of Xi and Putin might be a predictable result of the political systems in China and Russia, but similarly powerful leaders in democratic systems are an unwanted aberration. Would-be autocrats pose two hazards to democracy. They can take over the system and then distort it to make themselves indispensable, or they can direct their followers to tear down the system altogether.

Democracy cannot do away with leaders and remain responsive, and true democrats would not want to erode the connection between leaders and followers. Thus, democratic leadership is both structurally indispensable and potentially perilous. So long as leaders are willing to walk away from power, the system should remain resilient and durable. Individual leaders who presume themselves to be indispensable and then try to restructure political institutions to ensure they cannot be replaced constitute the greatest threat. We should be less concerned with what McCarthy and Meloni have done to gain power than with what they might do to keep it.

Notes

1 See Annie Karni, 'McCarthy Wins Speakership on 15th Vote After Concessions to Hard Right', *New York Times*, 7 January 2023, https://www.nytimes.com/2023/01/06/us/politics/house-speaker-vote-mccarthy.html.

2 See Luke Broadwater, 'Speaker Quest Reveals McCarthy's Tenuous Grip on an Unruly Majority', *New York Times*, 6 January 2023, https://www.nytimes.com/2023/01/06/us/politics/mccarthy-house-speaker-republicans.html.

3 See 'Too Much Is Being Expected of Mario Draghi', *The Economist*, 22 April 2021, https://www.economist.com/europe/2021/04/22/too-much-is-being-expected-of-mario-draghi.

4 See, for example, Tomaso Montanari, *Eclissi di costituzione: il governo Draghi e la democrazia* [Eclipse of the constitution: the Draghi government and democracy] (Milan: Chiarelettere, 2022).

5 See Elettra Ardissino and Erik Jones, 'Italy's Election Paradox', *Foreign*

Affairs, 21 September 2022, https:// www.foreignaffairs.com/europe/ italys-election-paradox.

6   See, for example, Ruth Ben-Ghiat, *Strongmen: Mussolini to the Present* (New York: W. W. Norton & Co., 2020); and Gideon Rachman, *The Age of the Strongman: How the Cult of the Leader Threatens Democracy Around the World* (New York: Other Press, 2022).

7   Here I draw heavily on both Rachman and Ben-Ghiat. See also Moisés Naím, *The Revenge of Power: How Autocrats Are Reinventing Politics for the 21st Century* (New York: St. Martin's Press, 2022).

8   See Liana Fix and Michael Kimmage, 'Putin's Last Stand: The Promise and Peril of Russian Defeat', *Foreign Affairs*, vol. 102, no. 1, January/February 2023, pp. 8–21; and Michael Jonsson and Johan Norberg, 'Russia's War Against Ukraine: Military Scenarios and Outcomes', *Survival*, vol. 64, no. 6, December 2022– January 2023, pp. 91–122.

9   See Tatiana Stanovaya, 'Can Putin's Center Hold?', *Foreign Policy*, 19 October 2022, https:// foreignpolicy.com/2022/10/19/ russia-putin-elites-threat-regime/.

10 See George Magnus, 'The Economic Consequences of Xi Jinping', *Survival*, vol. 64, no. 6, December 2022– January 2023, pp. 57–76; and Kevin Rudd, 'The World According to Xi Jinping', *Foreign Affairs*, vol. 101, no. 6, November/December 2022, pp. 8–21.

11 See Burhan Sönmez, 'Erdoğan: A Normal Man', in Vijay Prashad (ed.), *Strongmen* (New York: OR Books, 2018), pp. 39–48.

12 See Soner Cagaptay, 'Erdogan's End Game', *Foreign Affairs*, 4 January 2022, https://www.foreignaffairs. com/articles/middle-east/2022-01-04/ erdogans-end-game.

13 See Veronica Anghel, 'Together or Apart? The European Union's East– West Divide', *Survival*, vol. 62, no. 3, June–July 2020, pp. 179–202.

14 See G. John Ikenberry, 'Why American Power Endures: The U.S.-led Order Isn't in Decline', *Foreign Affairs*, vol. 101, no. 6, November/December 2022, pp. 56–73.

15 *Ibid.*, p. 60.

16 *Ibid.*, p. 71.

17 *Ibid.*, pp. 71, 73.

18 See E.H. Carr, *What Is History?*, 2nd edition (London: Penguin, 2008).

19 See Gautam Mukunda, *Indispensable: When Leaders Really Matter* (Boston, MA: Harvard Business Review Press, 2012).

20 See Erik Jones, 'Italy's Hard Truths', *Journal of Democracy*, vol. 34, no. 1, January 2023, pp. 21–35.

21 See Ikenberry, 'Why American Power Endures', p. 71.

22 See Maggie Haberman, 'After Dramatic 14th Vote, Trump Calls Holdouts Who Refused to Back McCarthy', *New York Times*, 7 January 2022, https://www.nytimes. com/2023/01/06/us/politics/trump- calls-gaetz-mccarthy.html.

23 See Gaetano Mosca and Hannah D. Kahn (trans.), *The Ruling Class* (New York: McGraw Hill, 1960).

24 Robert Michels, *Political Parties: A Sociological Study of the Oligarchical Tendencies of Modern Democracy* (New York: Free Press, 1962).

25 I wrote about this need for leadership in these pages almost 15 years ago. See Erik Jones, 'Elusive Power, Essential Leadership', *Survival*, vol. 51, no. 3, June–July 2009, pp. 243–51.

26 This is a central theme of Mukunda, *Indispensable*.

27 Naím, *The Revenge of Power*, p. xii.

28 See David A. Bell, *Men on Horseback: The Power of Charisma in the Age of Revolution* (New York: Picador, 2020), p. 9.

29 See Rachman, *The Age of the Strongman*, p. 10.